INDUSTRIAL LOCATION POLICY FOR ECONOMIC REVITALIZATION

INDUSTRIAL LOCATION POLICY FOR ECONOMIC REVITALIZATION

National and International Perspectives

Morris L. Sweet

PRAEGER SPECIAL STUDIES • PRAEGER SCIENTIFIC

Library of Congress Cataloging in Publication Data

Sweet, Morris L.
 Industrial location policy for economic revitalization.

 Bibliography: p.
 Includes index.
 1. Industries, Location of--United States.
2. Industry and state--United States. 3. Industries,
Location of. 4. Industry and state. 5. Investments,
Foreign. 6. Employees' representation in management.
I. Title.
HC110.D5S93   338.6'042'0973   81-2843
ISBN 0-03-052621-3   AACR2

Published in 1981 by Praeger Publishers
CBS Educational and Professional Publishing
A Division of CBS, Inc.
521 Fifth Avenue, New York, New York 10175 U.S.A.

© 1981 by Praeger Publishers

123456789   145   987654321

Printed in the United States of America

To My Wife
Sally

ACKNOWLEDGMENTS

The completion of this book was made possible by the generous contribution of persons, in the United States and overseas, who are too numerous to single for special recognition—colleagues, corporate officials, faculty, government officials, librarians, practitioners, researchers, specialists, and trade unionists. Wherever possible their names appear in the book, but the author is equally indebted to those who are not mentioned.

Portions of the book, which have been revised and expanded since their initial presentation, first appeared in papers prepared for annual meetings of the New England Business and Economic Conference, and articles in the July 1977 issue of Area Development, "Government Obstacles Mount When Expanding Overseas—Toyota's problems are resolved in England," and the Winter 1978-79 issue of Urbanism Past and Present, "Industrial Location Policy: Western European Precedents for Aiding U. S. Impacted Regions."

Permission to include the article from Area Development has been kindly granted, and "An in gratis reprint of Morris Sweet's article has been granted by Urbanism Past and Present of the University of Wisconsin-Milwaukee, Board of Regents, of the University of Wisconsin System, 1978."

The preparation, contents, and conclusions are the responsibility of the author and should not be ascribed to any organizations to which he is or has been affiliated.

CONTENTS

LIST OF TABLES AND MAPS

LIST OF MAPS

INDUSTRIAL LOCATION POLICY FOR ECONOMIC REVITALIZATION

1

INTRODUCTION

OBJECTIVES OF THE STUDY

This volume is concerned with government policies and programs that directly or indirectly control the locational pattern of industry and with their effects on industrial development and industrial
policy. The various forms of locational controls are indicative of
those becoming increasingly pervasive throughout the world. The examination of the controls is primarily from the standpoint of industrial
democracies as opposed to centrally planned economies. An objective
of this study is to analyze the locational impact of controls on industrial development nationally, regionally, and subregionally. In particular, the effect of controls on the recovery of depressed or declining economies within the framework of industrial policy or reindustrialization is examined.

Industrial development is defined in its broadest sense and is
not limited to manufacturing. The terms, location policy and regional
policy, are used interchangeably.

Direct controls are designed specifically for the purpose of requiring industry to select locations in accordance with stated government policy backed by legislation. These controls should be differen-
tiated from financial subsidies and incentives that are conditioned
upon compliance with governmental guidelines in which a firm remains
free to accept or reject and independently make a locational choice.
Indirect controls emerge from legislation, though not specifically
concerned with influencing location, that has a significant locational
component. The objective of this book is not to advocate more or less
intervention; rather it is to isolate and examine the economic impact
of the controls on private sector locational decisions.

1

In a number of the Western European countries where the legislation for direct controls already exists, business is restricted in its freedom to decide on locations outside the limits of government directives. Indicative of the locational impact inherent in indirect controls are codetermination and plant-closing legislation. Though not enacted with location as a major consideration, legislatively imposed codetermination gives employees a voice and a check on changes in location. The lack of codetermination in the United States does not indicate that it has been and will be without consequences in this country. The proposed plant-closing legislation, which is receiving much attention in the United States, would delay and increase the costs of closing or relocating a facility; an analysis of the impact on management and the national economy reveals differences in the results over the short and long run.

CHANGES IN THE ECONOMY

Locational decisions are a by-product of changes in the economy and in various industries. In prosperous periods expansions take place while concurrently other industries and firms are declining. In less prosperous periods the same process takes place in reverse.

> So long as the industrial system is subject to change, with the growth of new forms of activity to replace those which die away as demands and technique change, then we shall have the problem of the emergence of depressed areas. [1]

In periods of slow economic activity, the crucial problem is the curtailment or closing of facilities while there is limited growth in other sectors to absorb the newly idled resources. "If such a decline is now to affect a broad array of industries of economic and strategic importance . . . a more active government role in the adjustment will be called for."[2] However, it is not only in these periods that divestments and closings are significant. With rapid changes in technology and management having an increasingly wider choice of locations, the pace of closings is accelerated. Additional factors are the problems of inflation and energy costs.

Regional policy no longer can be limited or concerned solely with remedies for depressed regions but has to be made an integral part of facilitating change as well as mitigating the impact of change. A recurring theme in this volume is that this expanded version of regional policy cannot be viewed apart from national industrial policy. [3]

Regional policies, which were initially concerned with

measures to combat local unemployment caused mainly
by depressed industries, or because of persistent regional income disparities, have been developing rapidly
to encompass a broad range of economic and social policy
areas. As these regional policies assume a more active
and autonomous role, it becomes increasingly important
to understand the interactions between them and national
industrial policies so as to avoid possible inconsistencies
and conflicts. Policy developments in some countries represent an effort to place regional and national policies in
a common interrelated framework. [4]

What these diverse programs have in common is that they affect
industrial development and the location of industry by various means.
This book examines what could happen if similar programs were
adopted in the United States. The examination covers the involvement
of government, business and labor both domestic, foreign and transnational. In terms of location, what significant changes will be forthcoming from direct and indirect government intervention? How and
where will investments in facilities be made? How do these programs
fit in with the development of a national industrial policy?

CORPORATE FREEDOM

Throughout the world, industrial democracies either have placed
or are placing limitations on the freedom of industry to select locations unilaterally, but the United States is unique among advanced industrial democracies in that it "has made it a matter of practice—if
not, since 1970 of declared principle—to uphold the freedom of corporate choice" for mobility of enterprise. [5] An exception to this practice has been the imposition of government controls for reasons of
national security. The high degree of corporate freedom of mobility
in the United States has been the target of criticism for leading to a
variety of undesirable economic and social effects. [6]

A change in the policy of limited federal involvement in locational matters at the local level, could, if extended, limit the construction of industrial facilities and thus the corporate choice of sites.
Initially the applicability of the 1979 Community Conservation Guidelines is only for commercial development, but it could readily be extended to other sectors. According to the Guidelines issued by the
president of the United States, when local officials believe a federal
action taking place outside their communities could have significant
negative consequences, they can request the federal government to
delay these actions, e.g. assistance for highway access or sewer

facilities. [7] The Guidelines are a memorandum, not a law or executive order. The issue raised by the Guidelines and similar federal and state actions is whether the adoption of an economic impact rationale constitutes "an unprecedented preference for the economic vitality of one geographic area over another's, and when would it advance the welfare of the larger population. "[8]

The Guidelines are aimed at preventing development assistance from going to competing projects whose negative impact would be measured by loss of jobs, especially for minorities, reduction in the tax base, or loss of commercial enterprises. Shopping center developers and merchants contend that the policy is indicative of excessive large-scale federal intervention in land-use decisions which were regarded for many years as purely local decisions. [9] The policy introduces a land-use strategy directed to conserving existing communities. However the policy could readily be broadened to prevent an industrial firm from relocating, or to forestall developers from constructing an industrial park that would draw firms from their existing sites.

VALUE OF COMPARATIVE EXPERIENCE

This analysis of policies places great emphasis on comparing different foreign experiences, including both successes and failures. These experiences can be a source of new ideas which can be revised in the light of indigenous conditions. Failure elsewhere should not rule out the possibility of borrowing and adapting particular components or concepts. In addition to adaptation, an understanding of the foreign policies and programs becomes vital to participation of government, business, and labor in an increasingly interdependent world economy as reflected by the growth in world trade, importance of transnational corporations, international cooperation of trade unions, and activities of international governmental bodies.

NOTES

1. S. R. Dennison, The Location of Industry and the Depressed Areas (London: Oxford University Press, 1939), pp. 100-1.

2. U. S. , Congress, Joint Economic Committee, United States Long Term Economic Growth Prospects: Entering A New Era, 95th Cong. , 2d sess. , 1978, p. 63.

3. "The primary cause for the lack of economic development success, to date, is the fact that economic programs have been ameliorative, rather than developmental. They have tended to deal with the worst first: assisting firms on the verge of bankruptcy, for exam-

ple. The measures of success have not been the viability of the assisted firm, but technical measures such as was a loan repaid on time? In other words, programs have been measured in terms of bureaucratic criteria and they have not been targeted to economic goals of productivity, efficiency, employment and output (some of which, in some instances, are mutually exclusive)" "Draft Policy on Economic Development," APA Newsletter of the Economic Development Division 1 [July 1980]: p. 2).

4. Organization for Economic Cooperation and Development, The Aims and Instruments of Industrial Policy: A comparative study (Paris: 1975), p. 135.

5. James L. Sundquist, Dispersing Population: What America Can Learn from Europe (Washington, D.C.: Brookings Institution, 1975), p. 248.

6. Gerald L. Houseman, The Right of Mobility (Port Washington, N.Y.: Kennikat Press, 1979) pp. 39, 61-62.

7. U.S., President, "Community Conservation Guidelines," November 12, 1979.

8. Michael Fix, "Regional Malls and the Environmental Impact Process," Policy and Research Report Urban Institute 10 (Fall 1980): p. 8.

9. Housing and Development Reporter 7 (October 1, 1979): p. 376; 7 (November 26, 1979): p. 573; 7 (December 10, 1979): p. 845; Robin Lanier, "Analysis of the Administration's Community Conservation Guidance" in Lawrence A. Alexander, ed., Strategies for Stopping Shopping Centers: A Guidebook on Minimizing Shopping Center Growth (New York: Downtown Research and Development Center, 1980) p. 31; and Neal R. Pearce and Jerry Hagstrom, "White House Goes Downtown with Its Shopping Center Policy," National Journal 11 (November 17, 1979): p. 1943.

PART I

DIRECT CONTROLS

2

CONTROLS IN THE UNITED STATES

NEED FOR CONTROLS

As a solution to stemming and reversing the economic decline of impacted regions, little attention in the United States has been given to the feasibility of adapting national programs now functioning in other industrial democracies, notably Western Europe. The basis of these legislative programs is the limitation of industry's freedom to select locations of its choice and the directing of industry to targeted areas with severe economic problems. The direct controls prevent a company from establishing new or expanded facilities or to relocate without the approval of the government. The objective, which is usually linked to financial assistance, has not been only to improve economic conditions and reduce regional imbalances but also to decongest major urban centers. However, congestion is a less critical issue in the 1980s; it has never assumed the importance in the United States that it attained in Western Europe. Within the framework of locational controls, an aspect that is taking on major significance is the impact on productivity and efficiency.

The need for controls arises when financial incentives prove inadequate to direct industry to impacted regions. Ironically, in the United States the incentives tend to be greatest in areas where they are least needed in terms of stimulating regional economies. Locational controls do serve to differentiate among regions and could be more effective than financial incentives in placing facilities in the most troubled regions. Financial incentives in isolation may not be a sufficient inducement for industry to locate in target areas. Therefore, controls are necessary when firms are willing to forego financial benefits.

The diverse control legislation in four Western European countries provides a framework for an analysis of direct controls. Since these programs have been operational for an appreciable period, an examination and comparison of these experiences should provide an understanding of their overall viability as well as an indication of their applicability to the United States. The British and Italian programs may be most pertinent since they are national in scope, whereas the French and Dutch systems cover only particular regions within the country. Before examining the foreign programs, the limited United States experience with controls will be reviewed.

EMERGENCE OF CONTROLS

Government controls over the location of privately owned industrial facilities similar to those now in effect in Western Europe for nondefense purposes are not entirely unknown in the United States. Without specifying or selecting specific areas, the Department of Defense (DOD) has been in a position to affect the locational pattern of industry for many years. Direct controls emerged during the World War II period, and remained because of national security until the 1950s when they were discontinued due to changes in defense strategy; yet the power to guide locational decisions still remains. This chapter is not concerned with military bases and DOD-operated installations but rather with production by the private sector.

Before and during World War II, the Plant Site Board of the Office of Production Management (OPM) and its successor the War Production Board (WPB) determined defense plant locations. The Plant Site Board cooperated with the defense agencies in reviewing location applications and did not hesitate to withhold its approval when sites were considered unsatisfactory. The research staff examined all proposals with regard to the supply of labor, transportation, housing, power, materials, and the origin and destination of products. To the greatest extent possible, efforts were made to keep plants away from highly industrialized areas and placed in remote sites for strategic reasons. Furthermore, land could be obtained more readily in unpopulated areas. Many workers were forced to live in places where there was no community or merely a small town. [1]

> In the very beginning there was a spartan attitude which
> assumed that as part of the war effort the workers could
> be expected to live in tents and shanties. [2]

Though the Plant Site Board did perform a form of overall planning, it was done in a negative sense. The Board had no power to take the initiative, but it could make suggestions, reject proposals, or have them re-examined. Through these methods, the Board could influence plant location "which prevented . . . much undue concentration of industry."[3]

STRATEGIC RELOCATION

After World War II, the National Security Resources Act of 1947 established the National Security Resource Board (NSRB) as a permanent civilian agency to formulate "the strategic relocation of industries, services, government and economic activities."[4] The prevailing postwar strategy called for the dispersal of defense industries to protect them from strategic atomic attack. The underlying assumptions were: any future war would entail long attrition similar to World War II; atomic weapons delivered by aircraft would be used in small numbers; since industrial capacity would be the key feature in attaining victory, the side that could keep its industry intact and functioning would have the decisive advantage.[5] Based on these assumptions, considerable study and discussion took place within government and industry while the Korean War lent special impetus to measures to improve national military preparation. These considerations led to Section 2062 of the Defense Production Act of 1950 as amended which still gives legal form to the dispersion of defense industry.[6] The NSRB and later the Office of Defense Mobilization (ODM) assumed the leadership in promoting the dispersion of defense industry away from "probable target areas" which usually were large metropolitan areas. Useful dispersion was considered to be locating new industry 32 or more miles away from the centers of "probable target areas." Attempts were made to separate new industries from major military installations. For smaller urban areas and military bases, 15 miles away from their center was regarded as useful dispersion.

The customary procedure was to encourage industry to disperse but not to state specifically where; industry, not the Department of Defense, selected the sites. DOD was not involved with specific sites but had to review and certify that industry met dispersal standards. ODM certified the eligibility of industry for tax amortization. The greatest impact was on industrial production and some missile development sites but none on research facilities.

DE-EMPHASIS OF INDUSTRIAL DISPERSION

The industrial dispersion effort peaked between 1954 and 1956. In 1953, the first thermonuclear device exploded and shortly thereafter the ICBM program began. The linking of thermonuclear explosives with ballistic missiles raised questions about the strategic assumptions of the pre-hydrogen bomb era. It was no longer obvious that future wars would be fought along the lines of World War II, since the consequent fallout patterns would differ significantly from the atomic weapons patterns. [7]

Protection of industry would be much more difficult and expensive than previously assumed and the dispersion program had to be altered. "Industrial dispersion is a long-term proposition, and the rapid advance in capability of strategic delivery forces changed the rules of the game in midstream. In addition, nuclear weapons of all kinds were no longer as scarce as in the past. "[8]

The net affect of these strategic and technological changes was to de-emphasize the concern for industrial dispersion on the part of both government and industry, e.g. the tax amortization provisions were dropped in the late 1950s. [9] On the other hand there was increasing interest in incorporating socioeconomic considerations into defense procurement policies. It took the form of targeting federal procurement into areas of economic distress. There was an overlap during the Korean War when there was also a commitment to dispersion for defense production and defense mobilization purposes. The change came with the issuance of the 1952 Executive Order, Defense Manpower Policy No. 4 (DMP4), better known as the Labor Surplus Policy. Its purpose was to "provide for procurement by negotiated contracts and purchases with responsible concerns in an area of current or imminent labor surplus." Preference in federal contracts would be given to employers who would perform substantial portions of awarded contracts in areas classified as persistent or substantial unemployment areas. It was originally created to encourage full utilization of existing production facilities and their workers in contrast to the construction of new plants, thus maintaining economic balance and stability. In the revised policy, DMP4B of 1980, the Secretary of Commerce has the responsibility to urge concerns planning new production facilities to consider the advantages of locating in Labor Surplus Areas (LSAs). The Secretary also provides technical advice to organizations in LSAs planning industrial and commercial development. The LSA program has not been particularly effective in channeling government procurement to the designated areas. (See Tables 2.1 and 2.2.)

> The LSA program has been forced to compete with other
> socio-economic programs, such as those for small, mi-
> nority, and women-owned businesses, for the attention of
> procurement officials. Because the LSA program is the
> only one without an established full-time advocacy group

TABLE 2.1

Government Procurement and Labor Surplus Set-asides, 1972-76
(in millions of dollars)

Fiscal Year	Total Government Procurement	Labor Surplus Set-aside Procurements	Set-aside Procurement as a Percent of Total
1972	$45,204	$243	0.53
1973	44,742	302	0.68
1974	48,602	287	0.59
1975	58,544	175	0.30
1976	66,408	261	0.39

Source: U.S., General Accounting Office, The Labor Surplus Policy: Is It Effective In Providing Government Contracts To High Unemployment Areas And Jobs For The Disadvantaged?, PSAD-77-133, Washington, D.C., July 15, 1977, p. 6.

within the Federal government, agency procurement officers tend to give it a low priority. Weaknesses also are found in the program's procedures for oversight, goal setting, training, information, incentive and reporting systems, outreach, targeting mechanisms, and evaluation. Grants and cooperative agreements, a huge potential source of awards, have been dropped from the program, and the recently enacted international trade agreements endanger it by committing the United States not to discriminate against foreign firms in letting procurement contracts.[10]

AWARDING OF CONTRACTS

The Defense Department has consistently opposed the placing of contracts in Labor Surplus Areas to relieve unemployment. In opposition to DMP4 it claimed contracts could only be awarded to the lowest bidder and to low-cost locations. DOD officials have conceded to little or no interest in the regional economic consequences of the Department's procurement actions or in obtaining the data necessary to understand their implications.[11]

Before DMP4 could get off the ground its effectiveness was se-

TABLE 2.2

Defense Participation in the Labor Surplus Policy, 1952-76
(in millions of dollars)

Fiscal Year	Total Department of Defense Procurement[a]	Preference Awards[b]	Percent of all Defense Contracts
1952	$38,479	$41.6	0.11
1953	26,994	23.0	0.09
1954	10,632	8.5	0.08
1955	12,590	47.8	0.38
1956	14,320	4.2	0.03
1957	15,442	10.8	0.07
1958	18,725	36.6	0.20
1959	19,609	96.0	0.49
1960	18,439	22.3	0.12
1961	20,176	50.5	0.25
1962	22,964	106.1	0.46
1963	23,081	137.8	0.60
1964	23,048	172.9	0.75

Source: U.S., General Accounting Office, The Labor Surplus Policy: Is It Effective In Providing Government Contracts To High Unemployment Areas And Jobs For the Disadvantaged?, PSAD-77-133, Washington, D.C., July 15, 1977, p. 26 based on compilation by U.S. Department of Labor and the Department of Defense, Office of Assistant Secretary of Defense (Comptroller, Directorate for Information Operations).

[a]Excludes work performance outside the United States, includes

riously constrained by the passage in 1953 of the Maybank Amendment to the Defense Appropriations Bill. It required the Defense Department to buy goods at the lowest possible price and has been added routinely to every subsequent Defense Appropriations Bill. The first breach in the 27 year old Amendment came in December 1980 when the House and Senate agreed to a one year test program for fiscal 1981; $3.4 billion in defense contracts would be allocated to high unemployment areas. [12]

Over the years, members of Congress have disagreed with DOD's opposition to considering socioeconomic factors. In 1962, Senator Hubert Humphrey disagreed with the DOD policy of "the most

Fiscal Year	Total Department of Defense Procurement[a]	Preference Awards[b]	Percent of all Defense Contracts
1965	22,155	109.0	0.49
1966	30,824	98.2	0.32
1967	36,121	57.8	0.16
1968	35,921	108.4	0.30
1969	33,743	185.2	0.55
1970	28,623	135.5	0.47
1971	27,633	99.3	0.36
1972	30,093	208.8	0.69
1973	28,122	117.2	0.42
1974	30,086	103.8	0.35
1975	33,756	74.4	0.22
1976	36,561	153.0	0.41

civil functions. Excludes prime contracts under $10,000. Excludes construction and petroleum awards not subject to Labor Surplus Policy.

[b]Prime contract awards to large firms certified for preference under provisions of Defense Manpower Policy No. 4 include value of awards to subcontractors receiving a substantial proportion of a prime contract award received by certified prime contractor. Does not include awards under $10,000 or awards to small business with DMP-4 preference. Values are net values.

for the least money" as the relevant guide. He maintained that one can give nearly any area a strong research and development capability through the infusion of federal funds. "I realize it is difficult to get prime contracts in a distressed area, particularly if you have a policy that says: Well there is nobody to take care of it. There was nobody out in California to take care of it at first either. They put them there. . . . Anytime the Defense Department wants to make a going community they will do it."[13] He predicted that government would experience lower total costs, from decreases in unemployment insurance relief costs and gains in taxes from earned income, if contracts were channeled into Labor Surplus Areas.

Subsequently in 1976, Congressman William Moorhead of Pennsylvania commented: "Sure, we have defense manpower policy No. 4. But I think we would all agree that over the years it has not really been enforced. The military go where they want to go, and give only lip service to the requirement that they give consideration to procurement in areas of high unemployment. Shouldn't we be really pushing this kind of a policy to dampen these swings, these regional swings?"[14]

The officials in charge of the selection process for defense contracts have a degree of discretion over siting. Contracts have traditionally been the product of a process complex and uncertain enough to require negotiations rather than selection by formal advertising and low bid.[15] Negotiations open the way for inclusion of geographic considerations through awards.

PROCUREMENT AND REGIONAL GROWTH

The role of government procurement in regional growth from new industries, generally through negotiated contracts allowing for geographic discretion, is indicated by the government's sponsorship of successful innovation in new products and processes in research and development, and production. In addition, the government is a major customer for items such as computers, semiconductors, jet aircraft, nuclear power generators, telecommunications, pharmaceuticals and chemicals.

> Often, successful U. S. innovations . . . have been directly related to the U. S. government's role as an early large, and, above all, constant predictable customer for whatever it was that was being developed.
> . . . a few histories of great internationally competitive American innovations show an oft-recurring pattern of the U. S. government setting a defense or other priority, keeping to it over a period of years, and then getting industry to target its efforts at that priority by keeping the purchases coming (and perhaps by not being too finicky over cost-overruns and keeping to budget as long as basic objectives were met . . . but a short-term "budget" or financial mentality has appeared harmful to innovative productivity).[16]

Ruth M. Davis, Deputy Under Secretary of Defense for Research and Development, stated in 1978 that the Defense Department expects to program $100 million over the next five years for industrial innovation in optical lithography, fabrication techniques involving electron-beam technology, improved chip designing and testing to meet military specifications, system architecture and software implementation. [17] Once these contracts have been awarded, facilities constructed and equipment installed, the successful firm has an edge in obtaining subsequent contracts; the availability of the facilities and equipment plus the technical expertise gives it an inherent advantage over rival firms in obtaining further contracts in this product category. Paralleling the advantages to the successful firm are the long-range benefits that accrue to the area in which the facilities are placed.

The plans to rebuild the national economy on the basis of industrial or reindustrialization policy have tended to overlook the potential contribution from the defense sector. [18] For example, coordinating defense procurement and rebuilding infrastructure geographically would be important factors whereby industry is situated in the optimum location and regional economies are revitalized. Guiding or directing private sector locational decisions would be the unifying process through which this is accomplished.

NOTES

1. Ironically the Plant Site Board was directed to minimize the need for migration of workers, additional housing, and local services. U. S. , Civilian Production Administration, Bureau of Demobilization, Industrial Mobilization for War, History of the War Production Board and Predecessor Agencies, 1940-1945, Vol. 1, Programs and Administration— Historical Reports on War Administration (Washington, D. C. : Government Printing Office, 1947), p. 422.

2. David Novick, Melvin Anshen and W. C. Truppner, Wartime Production Controls (New York: Columbia University Press, 1949), p. 302.

3. Ibid. , p. 162.

4. Ibid. , p. 412.

5. Lt. Gen. William J. Ely, Deputy Director, Administration and Management, Office of Director of Defense Research, DOD in U. S. , Congress, Senate, Committee on Labor and Public Welfare, Subcommittee on Employment and Manpower, Impact of Federal Research and Development Policies on Scientific and Technical Manpower: Hearings, 89th Cong. , 1st sess. , 1965, p. 436.

6. "In order to insure productive capacity in the event of such an attack on the U. S. , it is the policy of the Congress to encourage the geographic dispersal of the industrial facilities of the U. S. in the interest of the national defense, and to discourage the concentration of such productive facilities within limited geographical areas which are vulnerable to attack by an enemy of the United States. In the con-

struction of any Government-owned industrial facilities, in the rendition of any Government financial assistance for the construction, expansion, or improvement of any industrial facilities, and in the procurement of goods and services under this or any other Act, each department and agency of the Executive Branch shall apply . . . when practicable and consistent with existing law and the desirability for maintaining a sound economy, the principle of the geographical dispersal of such facilities in the interest of national defense." U. S. Code, Vol. 5D, Sec. 2062.

7. Ely, Federal Research, p. 436.

8. Ely, Federal Research, p. 478.

9. The continued deemphasis of industrial dispersion was reconfirmed in 1976 by Jacques S. Gansler, Deputy Assistant Secretary of Defense for Material Acquisition: ". . . like dispersing of our industry, very clearly in terms of the Government-owned facilities, we can do that. In terms of the private sector . . . we have not been doing that. We have not been forcing them to put plants in certain areas. That is certainly getting heavily into the private sector." U. S. , Congress, Joint Committee on Defense Production, Defense Industrial Base: Industrial Preparedness and Nuclear War Survival: Hearings, Part 1, 94th Cong. , 2d sess. , 1977, p. 23.

10. Northeast-Midwest Institute, Targeting Federal Contracts: An Urban Policy Evaluation, (Washington, D. C.: September 1980), prepared by Diane DeVaul, p. ii.

11. Northeast-Midwest Institute, Federal Procurement and Regional Needs: The Case of Defense Manpower Policy Number Four (Washington, D. C.: March 28, 1977), prepared by Laurence Zabar, p. 1.

12. "Regions: West Gathers New Power in 1980; Industrial Sectors Lose Ground," Wall Street Journal, December 30, 1980, p. 17.

13. Hubert H. Humphrey in U. S. , Senate, Select Committee on Small Business, Impact of Defense Spending on Labor Surplus Areas: Hearings, 87th Cong. , 2d sess. , 1962, pp. 6, 7, 10, quoted in Roger E. Bolton, Defense Purchases and Regional Growth (Washington, D. C.: Brookings Institution, 1966), pp. 140-41.

14. U. S. , Congress, Joint Economic Committee, Subcommittee on Urban Affairs, Regional Economic Problems and National Economic Policy: Hearings, 94th Cong. , 2d sess. , 1977, p. 22.

15. Bolton, Defense Purchases, p. 2.

16. Lawrence G. Franko, "The Competitiveness of U. S. High-Technology Exports," testimony prepared for U. S. , Congress, Senate, Committee on Banking, Housing and Urban Affairs, Subcommittee on International Affairs, May 1978. (Recorded by witness.)

17. "Vanishing Innovations," Business Week, no. 2541 (July 3, 1978): pp. 52-53.

18. Under the Reagan Administration the cumulative Pentagon budget through fiscal 1986 could amount to more than $1.5 trillion and might even reach $1.5 trillion against $655 billion for the past five years. "Spending $1 trillion for stronger defense," Business Week, no. 2669 (December 29, 1980): p. 70.

3

CONTROLS IN GREAT BRITAIN

BACKGROUND

Geographic Boundaries

The locational controls systems have reached their apogee in Britain and thus offer the best model for an analysis of the effectiveness of the various systems. (See Table 3.1.) Regional development plans started in the 1930s as welfare measures to aid mining and industrial areas with high unemployment rates; subsequently, the emphasis was expanded to halt a population exodus from the depressed areas, encourage redevelopment of depressed areas, and to decongest urban centers, notably London. An integral part of the regional program is the national system of controls whereby, in conjunction with financial incentives, management is encouraged or required to place new or expanded industrial facilities in distressed areas. The degree of control and magnitude of financial aids vary by category of assisted area: special development, development and intermediate. The objective is to give the special development areas the greatest assistance to aid their recovery, while providing the least to the intermediate areas.

The boundaries were changed by the new Conservative Government in July 1979 and August 1980 with further changes due in August 1982. (See Maps 3.1 to 3.3). The Secretary of State for Industry intends to place a stronger emphasis on the needs of smaller assisted areas and to treat different areas of the country more consistently and equitably. His plan is to reduce the scope of the assisted areas from a point where in July 1979 they covered over 40 percent of the employed population to about 25 percent over a three-year period.

TABLE 3.1

Main Instruments of United Kingdom Regional Policy

Year	Policy	Major Provisions
1934	Special Areas (Development and Improvement Act)	Four Special Areas designated. Commissioners had powers to grant loans. Led to establishment of trading (industrial) estates. Powers extended in 1937.
1945	Distribution of Industry Act	Special Areas extended and designated as Development Areas. The wartime building license control was maintained. Grant and loan powers vested in the Board of Trade. Trading estate policy retained. Beginning of active phase of regional policy.
1947	Town and Country Planning Act	Introduced the Industrial Development Certificate (IDC) control with 5,000 sq. ft. limit. Subject to frequent modification and applied with varying stringency.
1950	Distribution of Industry Act	Small extension to loan and grant powers to assist mobile industry. The 1950s were a quiescent period for regional policy.
1967	Regional Employment Premium (REP)	Subsidy for employment in manufacturing industry in the assisted areas.
1967	Special Development Areas (SDAs) Development Areas (DAs)	Additional incentives in areas of greatest need. Rent free premises and additional building grants.
1970	Intermediate Areas	A new class of assisted area with lower rates of assistance than DAs and SDAs.

(continued)

21

Table 3.1, continued

Year	Policy	Major Provisions
1970	Budget	Investment Grants replaced by accelerated depreciation in assisted areas. Some relaxation of IDC limits.
1972	Industry Act	Regional Development Grants (RDGs) replaced the accelerated depreciation differential. IDCs abolished in DAs and SDAs and exemption limits raised elsewhere (10,000 sq. ft. in the southeast, 15,000 elsewhere). Regional selective assistance introduced.
1974	Regional Employment Premium	Rate of REP doubled. IDC limits tightened; 5,000 sq/ft. in southeast, 10,000 in other nonassisted areas.
1975	Development Agencies	Scottish and Welsh Development Agencies established. Responsible for factory building, powers to invest in industry.
1958	Distribution of Industry (Industry Finance) Act	Extension of areas eligible for assistance. Simultaneously IDC policy was applied with increased stringency.
1960	Local Employment Act	Repealed Distribution of Industry Act. Broad Development Areas replaced by Development Districts. New building grants were introduced.
1963	Local Employment Act	Introduction of standard investment and building grants.
1963	Budget	Free depreciation allowed for investment in assisted areas. Policy becoming far more active at this time.

Year	Policy	Major Provisions
1965	Control of Office and Industrial Development Act	Office Development Permits (ODPs) introduced for London and Birmingham, later extended. IDC limits were made more stringent in non-assisted areas.
1965	Highland and Islands Development Act	Established the Highlands and Islands Development Board. Extensive powers of grants, loans, and equity participation.
1966	Industrial Development Act	Development Districts replaced by broad Development Areas. Free depreciation replaced by a differential investment grant. Some easing of 1965 IDC limits.
1976	IDCs	IDCs limits eased: 12,500 sq. ft. in southeast, 15,000 in other non-assisted areas.
1977	Regional Employment Premium	REP abolished in GB.
1979	Revisions to Policy	Reduction in areas eligible for assistance. Rate of RDG reduced in DAs. Regional Selective Assistance to be more selective. IDC limits eased: 50,000 sq. ft. in nonassisted areas. ODCs discontinued.

Source: Judith Marquand, Measuring the Effects and Costs of Regional Incentives, Government Economic Service Working Paper no. 32 (London: Great Britain, Department of Industry, February 1980), pp. 17–18.

MAP 3.1

Britain—Assisted Areas, July 18, 1979

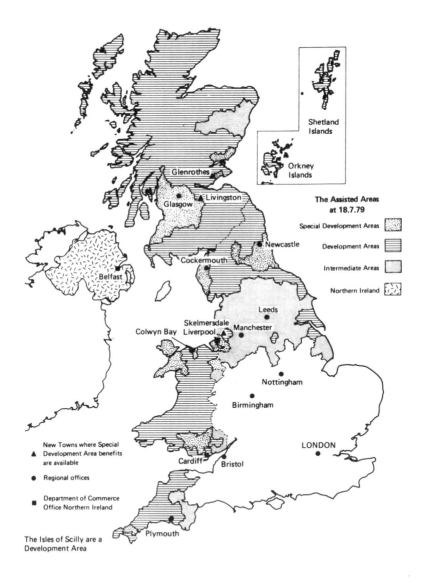

Glenrothes

Glasgow Livingston

Shetland
Islands

Orkney
Islands

**The Assisted Areas
at 18.7.79**

Special Development Areas

Development Areas

Intermediate Areas

Northern Ireland

Newcastle

Cockermouth

Belfast

Leeds

Skelmersdale Manchester
Colwyn Bay Liverpool

Nottingham

Birmingham

▲ New Towns where Special
Development Area benefits
are available

● Regional offices

■ Department of Commerce
Office Northern Ireland

The Isles of Scilly are a
Development Area

Cardiff Bristol

LONDON

Plymouth

Source: Great Britain, <u>Industrial Development Certificates</u>
(London: Department of Industry, September 1979).

24

MAP 3. 2

Britain—Assisted Areas, August 1, 1980

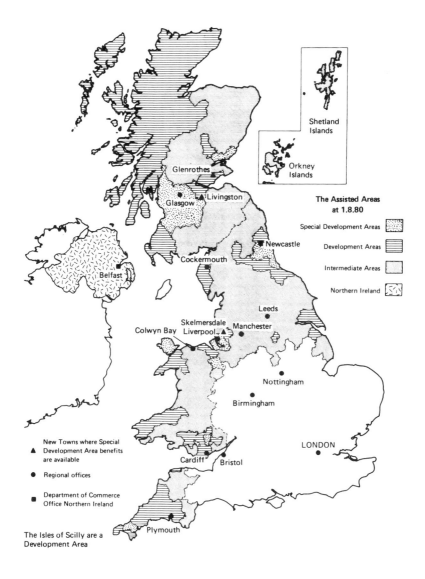

Source: Great Britain, Industrial Development Certificates
(London: Department of Industry, September 1979).

MAP 3.3

Britain—Assisted Areas, August 1, 1982

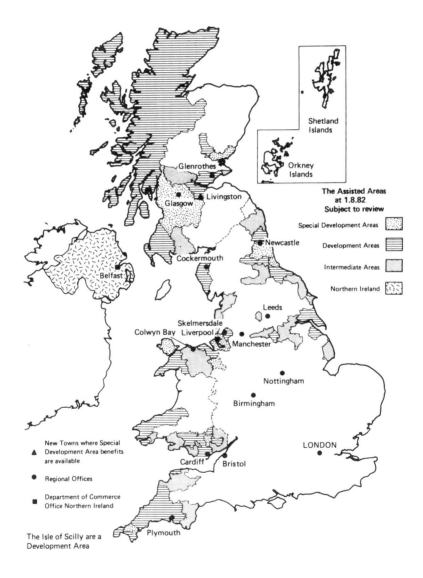

Source: Great Britain, Industrial Development Certificates (London: Department of Industry, September 1979).

Though not quite comparable (employed vs. total population), a very large proportion of the total population in the United States are also residents of what in British terms are assisted areas. In the hearings on the proposed National Public Works and Economic Development Act before the U. S. Congress in 1979, there was discussion on whether to reduce coverage of the national population from 70 to 61 percent. [1] Senator William Proxmire claimed that 85 percent of the total population in 1980 lived in officially designated distressed areas. [2]

Locational controls in the form of Industrial Development Certificates (IDCs) were initiated in 1947 to encourage manufacturing industry to locate in the assisted areas of Great Britain and Northern Ireland by controlling the location of new industry and the expansion of existing industry. The increasingly important service sector was regulated between 1965 and 1979 by the less stringent system of office development permits. They were required for any new office building over 30,000 square feet in London and Southeast England. The original intention was to prevent congestion in Central London. While in effect, permits for more than 75 million square feet of proposed office space were denied. Office development, following the demise of the permits, is controlled by the normal planning system. [3]

When IDCs Are Required

In Great Britain, IDCs are required only outside the assisted areas. They are necessary when the proposed development exceeds 50,000 square feet (4,645 square meters). After the IDC has been obtained, additional development up to the exemption limit is permissible without another application. Obtaining an IDC is a prerequisite for local planning permission, but does not guarantee that permission will be granted. IDCs are necessary for:

1. Construction or reconstruction of industrial buildings;
2. Extensions to existing buildings;
3. Alteration to existing buildings which results in the creation of additional industrial floor space;
4. Change of use of existing buildings from nonindustrial to industrial purposes;
5. Retention of industrial use when the use has been started without appropriate planning permission;
6. Retention of industrial buildings (or continuation of industrial use) without complying with the original conditions for which the IDC was granted.

The legislation mandates the Secretary of State to certify "that the development in question can be carried out consistently with the proper distribution of industry" and in arriving at a decision "have particular regard to the need for providing appropriate employment in the development areas."[4] Firms have to demonstrate that they cannot be reasonably expected to operate in the assisted areas. IDCs are designed to restrict factory construction in more prosperous regions and divert it to those in more urgent need of economic growth. The objective is to rectify economic imbalance among regions. IDC controls do not compel a firm to accept a specific location in special development or development area. Only when a firm wishes to expand does the government's veto power come into effect and the firm is restricted in its locational options.

The highest priority for mobile projects is assigned to the assisted areas followed by the partnership areas of inner London and inner Birmingham and then to the new and expanding towns.

Before submitting a formal application, informal discussions about the possibility of approval are permissible. There is no statutory right of appeal although the applicant can request an explanation for the refusal and request reconsideration.

CORPORATE EXPERIENCE

The best insights into the IDC process can be derived from the operational experiences and varied responses of firms whose locational decisions have been affected by the government's policy on granting IDCs. Their experiences and viewpoints would be a key consideration in considering any proposal to initiate locational controls in the United States.

IBM

The policy followed by IBM in Britain indicates that impacted regions could benefit from a long-term corporate strategy that considers the quality of the infrastructure instead of financial incentives to be the keystone of the locational decision. IBM's testimony revealed that the overriding consideration in a 1967 decision to locate a new plant was the proximity of a laboratory, a distance of a half-hour drive. The company wanted the staff associated with product design and development close by to activate the production line. If IBM had been unable to make use of an existing IDC, there would have been no investment in the United Kingdom. IBM considered the refusal of an IDC more important than the financial incentives. The incentives were balanced against the long-term view: the quality of labor and the infrastructure (communities, housing, schools). The firm would prefer that government expenditures be directed toward improving the infrastructure rather than attempting to attract firms via direct financial incentives. The IBM official stated:

> . . . there are three main factors to be considered in terms of major IBM investment anywhere. First there is the infrastructure of the locality and I include in that roads, communication, airports, schools and housing. Secondly there is the availability of labor and you have to bear in mind that we do employ a high percentage of qualified people. Thirdly there are the costs associated with the particular location and regional incentives form part of the third factor. Taking a long term view . . . we believe that the infrastructure is infinitely more important than the actual cost involved at any particular time. It is the infrastructure which helps to attract people to the locality and keep them there. [5]

He further stated that the government has a responsibility to ensure that the infrastructure is satisfactory so the benefits of new technology can be optimized. The company does not subscribe to the view that there is government and there is industry and the "two are separate and their paths shall never cross. "[6] The barriers are being broken down all the time and the company has to work closely with government to identify the responsibilities of both industry and government.

IBM's contention that it had to locate near a research establishment was considered highly suspect by a specialist in multinationals, Stuart Holland of the University of Sussex. [7] He contended that the case for research by a U. S. multinational in the United Kingdom was overstated and that IBM secures cost savings from widely dispersed production rather than by clustering around research centers. Furthermore, IBM's case for proximity was contradicted by its statement that ". . . a particular computer installation in one country today might consist of some peripheral units made in Greenock [UK] and Sweden linked up with a central processing unit made in Havant, Germany or France linked up with some other equipment made in Italy perhaps. It is quite a complicated rationale but we do obtain economies of scale from that mode of operation. "[8] Dr. Holland conceded that there was a strong case for IBM's greater stress on social infrastructure over financial incentives as a locational determinant.

Burroughs

As contrasted to the IBM policy, a major factor in the determination of locations for Burroughs within Great Britain has been the
financial incentives which in turn have led to sites in development
areas. The ultimate decision on investment is made in Detroit where
specific locations are not deemed overly important. Probably the critical consideration in making the ultimate locational decision would
have to be the financial incentive. In view of this selection process,
obtaining an IDC presents no problem.

Honeywell

Honeywell is an example of a company that successfully located
in a development area and, like Burroughs, has found the financial
incentives to be major factors in persuading the company to locate in
the United Kingdom rather than elsewhere in Europe.

The firm's products require a fairly low proportion of labor input. Such high technology industry relies less on semi-skilled and
craft labor and increasingly on design engineers, automated assembly
equipment and miniaturized components. Honeywell would like to see
the government reinforcing efforts to attract companies providing
components and other supplies to development areas.

Unilever

A rational corporate locational policy that might be beneficial
for maintaining industry in declining areas is followed by Unilever.
It indicates a high degree of corporate responsibility to shareholders,
employees, and communities with Unilever plants.

> The comparatively small number of factories built on new
> sites over the past twenty years is illustrative of the great
> advantages in most cases of developing on an existing site.
> This will often be true irrespective of whether the factors
> which originally governed the choice of location still apply.
> Where an investment takes the form of replacing, modern-
> izing or expanding a factory, it would require an impracti-
> cably high level of subsidy to make it worthwhile to relocate
> the whole plant. [9]

The reliance on existing sites is based on a long-range policy
of not deferring maintenance; therefore, when a decision has to be

made concerning the retention or abandonment of facilities, the expenditures required to retain the facility is not so exorbitant that only abandonment is feasible. [10] The company finds it difficult to demonstrate that regional subsidies for investment or employment have other than a small effect on their locational decisions. Unilever has conceded that even though incentives are of marginal importance, they do increase the profitability of investment. [11] The question arises as to whether even Unilever would remain in an area with a rapidly deteriorating infrastructure.

Ford

Ford, like other automobile manufacturers, found that added costs were incurred from locations in development areas. They arose from a lack of labor efficiency during the early stages of the operation, and from higher freight, travel, communication, and training costs.

In areas with a long heritage of industrial depression and unemployment, Ford found it necessary to recruit, train, and supervise a large number of workers with little or no experience in a mass production industry where work standards are confined to piecework payments. There is no evidence that, in terms of physical fitness, general education, and intelligence, these employees are not equal to those outside of development areas. Performance in turns of turnover, attendance and labor disputes tends to be less satisfactory than in established plants. The symptoms of adjusting the labor force to new technology are illustrated by the tendency for better relations in machinery operations than in assembly line operations.

Ford asserts that the poor profit record of the motor industry in past years has been partly due to the increasing proportion of uneconomic operations in the development areas. Though Ford received £13 million in grants for investment in development areas between 1962 and 1972, it would have done without the grants if expansion could have been on the sites it preferred outside of development areas. [12] On an annual basis the net annual recurring penalty costs to Ford due to plant dispersal into development areas was estimated by the company to be £130,000. (See Table 3.2.)

The largest item, freight costs, was attributed to scattered facilities; a less costly and integrated facility in one place would have been preferred by the company. The next largest item, travel and communications, represented the added costs from separate facilities for travel, telephone and telex services. The benefit from the investment grants of £13 million were not amortized nor used as a reduction of the penalty costs; Ford considered them completely offset by

TABLE 3.2

Ford Motor Company—Net Annual Recurring Penalty Costs
Due to Disperal into Development Areas
(in thousands of pounds)

Costs		
Freight	£900	
Travel and Communications	200	
Staff Relocation	70	
Additional Training	30	
Distribution	(100) reduction	
Inventory (in shipment)	30	
Total		£1,130
less		
Annual Regional Employment Premium	1,000	1,000
Net Annual Recurring Penalty Costs		£ 130

Source: Great Britain, House of Commons, Expenditure Committee, Trade and Industry Subcommittee, Regional Development Incentives, Minutes of Evidence from October 1972 to June 1973 and Appendices, 327, Session 1972-73 (London: Her Majesty's Stationery Office, 1973), p. 82.

the considerably higher penalty costs experienced in the early years of operations at the new locations.[13] The Department of Trade and Industry commented that there was no consideration by Ford of the capital allowances available against taxes.[14] A time factor has to be applied against these figures; Ford conceded that expansion could not have continued to take place on one site since there is a maximum or optimum size to any one complex.[15]

Despite its previous critical assertions about development areas, Ford decided to place its huge £80 million engine plant in a development area in South Wales. An unprecedented level of government financial assistance was a key factor in the decision. Though Ford was concerned about poor British labor relations and productivity, wage levels at least 50 percent below those in Germany were compensation for deficiencies. Also South Wales offered good communications, a ready supply of labor due to closings in steel mills and coal mines, and a large cleared site ready for construction.

TOYOTA: A CASE HISTORY OF CONTROLS

How do foreign firms react to locational controls? How do national governments respond to internal conflicts and opposing local interests? The case of Toyota provides insight into the multifaceted problems and the competing interests encountered in gaining compliance of controls by foreign firms. What is the corporate response to suggestions for moves to locations considered undesirable? How important are financial subsidies in affecting the corporate location decision?

Company Plans

Toyota had been importing automobiles through Sheerness in Southeast England and distributing them through centers in Croydon, a part of Greater London, and Crawley, which is south of London, and in 1976 decided to consolidate its operations in Bristol. The facility was to be utilized for parts storage, an import depot and administrative headquarters to handle imports of 30,000 cars per year. A £5,500,000 base was planned for the West Dock in Bristol where new cars would be dewaxed and minor repairs made on cars damaged in marine transit. Toyota did not anticipate any problems obtaining an IDC. But the Government contended the proposed degree of car assembly in the operation was over 15,000 square feet of manufacturing space and an IDC was necessary unless the facility was placed in a development area. The contention was that there would be assembly work, apparently referring to the removal of the protective wax applied prior to shipment from Japan. Toyota in turn countered that an IDC was really not necessary since the import center was primarily a warehouse and claimed the removal of the wax is no more a production process than removing wrapping paper from a parcel. In addition, the dewaxing plant did not exceed 15,000 square feet, and therefore was below the size mandating an application for an IDC.

The Government added fuel to the controversy by tying in the grant of an IDC to the location of the Toyota facility in an area of high unemployment, preferably Merseyside (Liverpool), South Wales, or Northeast England. Substantial financial incentives, reputedly £1 million, from the government for a move to a development area, were involved.

Toyota responded that it was not interested in regional grants and a move to Liverpool would entail higher costs and more serious inconveniences than a Bristol site. Key workers would not consider moving to Liverpool; the company "has over the years built up a highly professional managerial key staff whom it would be absolutely essentialy to retain." They simply could not be replaced and "they are of a calibre to seek and obtain employment anywhere without difficulty. These managers bluntly like things as they are; while we could probably persuade most of them to come to the West Country [Bristol], provisional soundings on Liverpool are emphatic. They would not consider it and it is not just a matter of inducements."[16]

If the approval by the government were not forthcoming, the company stated it might abandon the plan to expand in the United Kingdom and continue to use present facilities. "We are not interested in government assistance and we chose Bristol for purely economic reasons. If we cannot go to the West Dock, we might as well stay where we are."[17] "We are not interested in any kind of financial inducements to move where we do not want to go. We prefer to finance our own operations."[18] The Bristol location had been selected only after a most thorough search of alternatives.

Ironically, at the same time a number of other major Japanese concerns with sizable operations in the United Kingdom settled in development areas to their great satisfaction: NSK, ball bearings;[19] National Panasonic, color television; Matsushita, electronics; YKK, zip fasteners; Takiron, PVC plastic sheeting; and Sony, television. It should be noted that the facilities were not in inner cities. Toyota's reluctance to consider Liverpool favorably could be comprehended in view of the city's long standing negative image.

One of the chief reasons for the willingness of Japanese compa-

TABLE 3.3

Port of Bristol Trade and Revenues

Fiscal Year	Trade (millions of tons)	Revenues (£ millions)	Surplus (Loss) (£ millions)
1974	5.8	9.3	0.2
1975	5.3	10.6	(0.1)
1976	4.1	12.0	0.6
1977	4.2	15.0	1.5
1978	4.2	14.7	(3.4)
1979	4.4	17.3	(5.8)
1980	4.8	19.8	(7.7)

Source: William Hall, "Trying to be shipshape and in fashion," Financial Times, August 2, 1980, p. 17.

nies to go into development areas is that they "are used to a degree of Government 'guidance' and once one moves, others follow."[20]

The incumbent Labor government found itself beset with internal conflict with members of Parliament (MPs) coming from both Liverpool and Bristol strongly favoring their respective areas. Among the MPs from Bristol were the Energy Secretary, Mr. Anthony Wedgewood Benn and the Government Chief Whip, Mr. Michael Cocks.

However, the Labor Minister of State for Industry, Mr. Alan Williams, citing an unemployment rate of 16 percent in Liverpool, which was double that of Bristol, claimed that the Toyota investment is mobile and could materially aid a development area such as Merseyside. The Minister asserted: "If an industry becomes available for location and is sufficiently footloose to be steered into an assisted area, then we make every effort to do so."[21] The second priority for directing industry was to new towns.

The Economist raised the question as to whether the tough government tactics were designed "to keep Japanese cars from flowing in faster."[22]

Opposition by Bristol

Bristol built the West Dock with local financing without any national government assistance at a cost of £37 million. Supposedly the Labor Party attempted unsuccessfully either to stop construction of West Dock in the late 1960s, or to nationalize it and therefore wanted to retaliate. Local officials feared that if Toyota took its £5 million complex elsewhere, the new £37 million West Dock paid for by local taxpayers would be uneconomical. A rejection of Toyota could deter other firms from considering a Bristol location which had about 20,000 people unemployed. Toyota was the first firm customer for space at the dock. A spokesman for the Port of Bristol Authority stated: "Just as we land our first fish the smart alecs in Whitehall want to snatch it away from us."[23]

Bristol is in a good geographical position in relation to London and Birmingham and has diversified types of industrial space, e.g. the Concorde was built there. But in view of the losses subsequently incurred by the port, there was justification for the strong campaign to keep Toyota in Bristol. (See Table 3.3.)

Concern for Liverpool

A reputed reason for the national government's concern with a Liverpool location was the need to help the ailing Royal Seaforth complex which cost the government £50 million. It opened in 1971 and reportedly was losing £2 million annually, largely because the container terminal was operating at half capacity and was costing the Government about £5 million in annual interest costs. Thus, occupancy by Toyota would have appreciably improved the financial position of the controlling Mersey Docks and Harbour Company.

Liverpool handled a large share of British Leyland exports to North America as well as the imports of Italian Fiats. It could offer regular car ferry service to Ireland.

A group of Merseyside Labor MPs asserted that the Port of Bristol Authority offered Toyota "a cheap deal" to set up the car complex at the West Dock and a move to Bristol would instigate a price-cutting war between ports in the country. The Port of Bristol Authority denied that their rates were uneconomic but instead were highly competitive. [24]

Editorial Comment

Several of the national newspapers which tended to be critical of the Labor Government were scathing in their comments on the imposition of restrictions on Toyota. Their comments indicate the importance placed on regional economics.

> Why should Bristol, with its relatively good industrial relations, suffer—to the problematical benefit of less responsible people elsewhere? It will not in the long run (or even in the comparatively short run) benefit Merseyside or the North-East. "Regional policy"—with its tendency to preserve unproductive jobs and prop up unprofitable industries for political reasons—can never do that. It will also drive away investment from these shores. [25]

> If the government allows this Gilbertian situation to continue, people will again be prompted to ask whether there is any point in continuing to force industry into areas where economically speaking, it makes no sense for them to be . . . whether ministers are prudent to risk another rebuff over such a time-consuming, expensive and bureaucratic business as that of pushing industrialists into areas where they have no wish to be. [26]

An August 25, 1976 Daily Telegraph editorial suggested that there are reasons other than concern with the need of depressed areas for the Labor Government's position. They are an intense fear of multinationals because they cannot be controlled by the Labor group; "protectionist, or siege-economy attitudes" to protect the state-supported British domestic auto industry, regardless of competitive ability; and dislike of foreigners or, at least, successful capitalist foreigners. [27]

The more liberal magazine, New Society, commented that the dispute between Bristol and the Secretary of Industry over Toyota "has opened up a running sore in regional policy" and was as critical as the more Conservative journals on the government's regional policy and industrial strategy: "Judging by current indicators, it isn't working—or it doesn't exist. "[28]

Resolution of Location Dispute

After all the controversy, the resolution seems almost anticlimactic. To support its decision to locate in Bristol, Toyota rescaled their industrial needs to 14,990 square feet of floor space with the help of their architect while projecting a decline in marine damage attributable to import. The revised application was submitted to the Secretary of State for Industry who granted approval.

The Toyota experience indicates how difficult it is to administer location controls in the face of competing political factions, even within the same party, representing the economic interests of their constituencies. Regional policy can be used to support a national economic policy, e.g. to limit imports. The failure of the government demonstrates how a company in a strong bargaining position can afford to ignore the availability of generous financial subsidies. The reliance on financial incentives to direct firms to designated areas may not be sufficient by itself but must be buttressed by strong locational controls.

INMOS: A SOURCE OF INDUSTRIAL REVITALIZATION?

As this book is being completed, a complex series of events with overlapping political, economic, regional and technological elements is unfolding. The outcome of this process hinges to a large extent upon a decision for the location of facilities. [29]

The industrial backwardness of Britain has long been attributed to a lack of technological progress and overdependence on imported technology. As a major component of its industrial policy hopefully leading to a revitalization of the British economy, the government has selected the semiconductor industry. Negotiations have been held with the Anglo-American enterprise, Inmos, to produce microchips initially and eventually microprocessors. Inmos plans to manufacture chips in large quantities for a wide range of applications in computers, tele-communications, and industrial controls.

After months of argument in 1978, the Department of Industry reluctantly conceded it could not compel Inmos under the wing of the National Enterprise Board (NEB) to place its main microchip facility in a development area. The company received a $60 million subsidy to be used primarily for a U. S. factory in Colorado Springs. A second $60 million subsidy was delayed pending resolution of the conflict over the location of the British facility; a request for a third $60 million was anticipated.

The major obstacle to granting the second $60 million subsidy and continuing the project was the delay in settling the dispute over where the Inmos British facility should be placed. The company preferred to be in Bristol where it already had a technical center, rather than accede to the strong pressure to select a site within a development area. There was no unanimity within the government. According to Prime Minister Margaret Thatcher, if Inmos were to receive the second $60 million, the factory should be in South Wales; yet, the Secretary of State for Industry, Sir Keith Joseph, continued to express a strong preference for Bristol.

The controversy continued into 1980 with Welsh and Scottish ministers insisting that any new money from NEB be predicated on the plant being in a depressed region rather than in Bristol. Most Cabinet ministers preferred that the factory, which would employ 3,000 people, be placed in an area of high unemployment with Cardiff in Wales the favored site. But the company continued to stand firm for its choice:

> But Inmos founders have their hearts set on the bucolic environs of Bristol, and they refuse to be budged. They argue that the "silicon superstars" Inmos has attracted want to wake up to vistas of rolling green hills, not to a gray industrial landscape. The company has already picked out a site where it is ready to begin construction. [30]

The government resolved the issue by approving the second $60 million subsidy in July 1980 and deciding that the plant would be in South Wales where there were several alternative factories available. Approximately 2,000 new jobs over the next three to four years were anticipated. By 1985, there would be about 1,650 jobs in a second United Kingdom production plant in an assisted area. Another 1,500 jobs could result in Britain with suppliers to Inmos.

In contrast to Toyota's firm stance, largely due to its ability to refuse government financial aid, Inmos is highly dependent on subsidies and therefore could not resist pressure to locate in a depressed area. The resolution of the controversy should provide a precedent for determining whether high technology industries, and research and development operations can be successful in development areas. The French government recognizes the difficulties involved in placing such activities in depressed regions. [31]

The political controversy over funding and location tends to obscure the basic question of the marketability and profitability of the Inmos products. Approximately forty well-established companies throughout the world are already in this field. If industrial policy is to succeed, these high-risk industries often can be fostered and nurtured only through generous public financial assistance. Will management still be free to make locational decisions and ignore regional considerations despite the government aid?

SURVEY FINDINGS

Factors in Choice of Sites

A British government-sponsored survey of 543 firms opening new manufacturing plants from 1964 to 1967 revealed that labor was the principal factor in the choice of a location and IDCs were next. Respondents were interviewed and asked whether the factors shown in Table 3.4 were major or minor. The factors were not mutually exclusive.

The availability of an IDC and the labor factor were considered more significant by foreign-owned firms than by domestic firms. The variation between the foreign and domestic firms is even greater since the percentages for all firms includes the foreign firms. Although the survey took place in the mid-1960s, the findings may still hold true.

Refusals of IDCs

A survey of 1,369 firms that were refused IDCs between 1958 and 1971 disclosed that 18 percent subsequently established plants in assisted areas, or locations acceptable to the government; 25 percent met their needs by building a more modest extension, usually below the exemption limit, or by using ancillary space not requiring an IDC; 25 percent overcame the refusal by acquiring existing vacant space locally; 6 percent solved their problem by rationalizing and reorganizing production; and 13 percent abandoned the project, although this was not necessarily due to the refusal of an IDC. (See Table 3.5.) Actually 20 to 25 percent of those receiving IDCs subsequently fail to carry out the project. [32]

TABLE 3.4

Factors in Choosing a Location by 543 Firms Opening
New Manufacturing Plants, 1964-67

Factor	Percentage of Responses			
	Major[a]	Minor[a]	Major[b]	Minor[b]
Labor	72	20	76	18
IDC	48	18	56	10
Govt. Inducements	39	7	51	10
LA-etc., assistance	36	30	32	34
Transport	31	20	57	17
Markets	30	14	35	13
Amenities	29	41	30	45
Non-Govt. Factory	28	5	21	7
Managerial	24	17	17	13
Site Characteristic	20	17	23	17
Supplies	15	14	15	16
Services	3	5	5	3
Other	12	2	13	2
Premises				
(govt. or non-govt.)	38	6	35	10

Source: Great Britain, House of Commons, Expenditure Committee, Trade and Industry Subcommittee, Regional Development Incentives, Minutes of Evidence, July 1973, Appendices and Index,
85-1, Session 1973-74 (London: Her Majesty's Stationery Office,
1973), p. 600.
[a]All cases
[b]Overseas Ownership
LA—Local Authority

In practice most applications are now approved. Reasons for
the small number of rejections are that firms will not formally apply
if they anticipate a refusal, and the government has relaxed IDC controls. According to the Annual Report of the Secretaries of State for
Industry for the period, April 1, 1978, to March 31, 1979, 1,423
IDCs for schemes of 15,000 square feet and over in special development and development areas were issued, which resulted in an estimated additional employment of 55,910 people covering 60,925,000
square feet. There were nine refusals of schemes totaling 518,000 square

feet of industrial floor space. Seven of the nine refusals were in Southeast England which includes the Greater London Council area. [33]

TABLE 3.5

Actions Taken by Firms Following IDC Refusal, 1958-71

	Firms		Space Refused	
	Number	Percent	Sq. Ft. (1,000's)	Percent
Totals	1,369	100.0	45.0	100.0
Moved to location preferred by the government	251	18.0	12.0	27.0
Assisted area	(122)	(9.0)	(7.2)	(16.0)
Overspill/new town	(71)	(5.0)	(2.3)	(5.0)
Other	(58)	(4.0)	(2.5)	(6.0)
Developed in area originally chosen or in other non-preferred area	683	50.0	19.5	43.0
In existing premises	(340)	(25.0)	(10.1)	(22.0)
By building	(343)	(25.0)	(9.4)	(21.0)
Rationalization/ reorganization	84	6.0	2.9	6.0
Abandoned the project	176	13.0	6.1	14.0
Firm subsequently closed before taking any action	29	2.0	0.5	1.0
Developed abroad	7	1.0	0.2	1.0
Miscellaneous	25	2.0	0.5	1.0
Insufficient information	114	8.0	3.3	7.0

Source: Great Britain, Department of Industry, Some Aspects of the Impact of Industrial Development Certificate Policy, from Reinhart Wettman et al., Deglomeration Policies in the European Community: A Comparative Study (Berlin: International Institute of Management, 1978), p. 204a.

EVALUATION OF IDCs

Impact on Development Areas

Evaluations of IDCs indicate that they have had a positive impact on investment and employment in the development areas. Attempts to evaluate IDCs must contend with the problems of inadequate information, [34] a lack of goals by which to measure progress, [35] and an inability to separate improvements resulting from regional policy as a whole versus those attributable to individual policy measures like IDCs. For example, variations in the stringency of IDC controls have been accompanied by similar changes in financial incentives, making it a formidable task to reach conclusions about the effects of either.

The importance of government policy is evidenced by: the appreciable improvement in an area's competitive position when it is designated as a development area; the ensuing benefits from the refusals of IDCs elsewhere; and the eligibility for financial inducements. The development areas in Scotland attracted a larger volume of "immigrant" industry than could be expected from their share of Scotland's total unemployed, [36] but "if the Government had not operated a policy of control and inducement, the amount of freely chosen movement to the assisted areas would have been extremely small. "[37]

Controls and Incentives

According to A. J. Brown of the University of Leeds, the best generalization that can be made is that IDCs and incentives have acted together to produce effects greater than the sums of either operated in the absence of the other. [38] His analysis of variance growth models for the periods 1953-59 and 1961-66 indicates that something beside changes in structure and performance of industries caused an increase in growth and this was largely due to the strengthening of regional policy:

> . . . between these two periods, potential employment in
> moves to the assisted regions increased by about 15,000
> a year, and the number of new jobs in IDCs approved in
> them increased in relation to the rest of the country, by
> some 30,000 a year or more, which would eventually bring
> with them something like an extra 20,000 a year in local
> service industries. It seems likely . . . that most of the
> change of pattern in moves and approvals was due to the
> strengthening of policy. If this is granted, it is very hard
> to suppose that the improvement in the relative performance

of the assisted regions (after eliminating structural factors) was not the result of strengthened policy also. [39]

Brian Ashcroft and Jim Taylor of the Universities of Strathclyde and Lancaster found that both incentives and controls had a significant impact on the movement of manufacturing industry between 1961 and 1971.

> . . . our analysis of the effect of regional policy on movement of industry to development areas suggests a substantial role for location controls which have clearly been the backbone of the redistribution of industry policy. Investment incentives also played a crucial role in inducing firms to the development areas and special development areas. [40]

They conclude in a later article that the shift of industry to development areas relies heavily upon the aggregate movement of industry. In turn this movement seems to rely upon the total level of investment spending. A prerequisite for directing industry into the development areas could be locational controls and capital subsidies though they are not deemed sufficient, per se. [41]

Other analysts have attempted to measure IDC policy on the basis of refusals. Taking into account the probable underestimation of the impact of IDC policy due to the firms who do not apply because they anticipate rejection, Moore and Rhodes of Cambridge University found that "the effects of IDC policy . . . may be substantial."[42] They estimate that between 1960 and 1970, an estimated 120,000 jobs in prosperous areas were affected by refusals. This represents over one-third of the estimated additional employment related to completions in development areas. "Whether a refusal in a prosperous area subsequently becomes an approval in a Development Area is . . . a matter of some uncertainty although there is some evidence from surveys to suggest that this does occur to a limited extent."[43]

In a subsequent reassessment, Moore and Rhodes found that regional policy had been considerably weakened and therefore was less effective in the 1970s than in the 1960s, but the policy continued to create jobs though at a slower rate than in the 1960s.[44] They confirmed their earlier findings that IDC and investment incentive policy make a significant contribution to the movement of industry to development areas. They found that the strength of IDC policy had been substantially reduced by 50 percent in the 1970s as compared to the 1960s average. A by-product of the weakening was an estimated loss of 2,000 to 2,500 jobs in development areas per annum. The important financial inducements, regional employment premium and investment incentive, were also weakened during the 1970s. Another factor was that the continued decline in manufacturing employment nationally, which was due to limited investment, further reduced the effectiveness of regional policy; there were fewer mobile projects that could go to the development areas.

BUSINESS OPINIONS

A Political and Economic Planning (PEP) survey with a different approach than the aforementioned studies concurs on the importance of IDCs as a locational determinant. [45] The survey sought to examine individually the role of major government policies, such as IDCs, based on the opinions of business firms.

Profile of Firms

Of the 255 factories established in Special Development Areas in England and Wales between 1973 and 1976, 62 were opened by new firms from outside the area of the new facility. The 62 factories represented more than 80 percent of total new manufacturing employment. Seven of the 62 firms were controlled by parent companies in the United States. The survey responses were based largely on unstructured meetings and were not geared to produce answers of a statistical nature.

Ten percent or 16 firms said that actual or expected IDC refusal had effectively restrained their locational choice. [46] Five of the 16 firms said that had there been no IDC controls they would have expanded at their existing sites in the Southeast or the Midlands; three firms that lacked space for expansion would have expanded at other locations in the same region; one foreign company would have preferred a location in the Southeast; and one firm would have moved out of London but not to a development area.

There were certain similarities in the responses. The nine British firms mentioned shortage of space at their existing location as the major reason for wanting to open a new facility; seven of these firms were looking when vacant space was scarce in Southeast England and the Midlands. Seven firms would have experienced some difficulty in finding suitable space because of a need for special features. Even in the absence of IDC approval, the companies that wanted to expand had little choice other than moving to a development area. IDCs affected only a minority of firms but the impact was critical from a regional standpoint because the new factories built by this group were among the largest, accounting for 28 percent of total anticipated employment. [47]

Effectiveness of IDC Controls

The conclusion was that IDC controls with reservations serve to bring jobs to areas where they are needed. "Thus it may reasonably be concluded that IDC controls, where they operated, were highly effective and that in their absence significantly fewer jobs would have gone to the special development areas. It would thus seem a useful control to continue."[48]

Weaknesses of IDC Controls

Granting or refusing an IDC inevitably involves civil servants in the Department of Industry who have the difficult job of judging the feasibility of locating an activity in a development area. Often the judgments made must seem arbitrary or ill-advised to the applicant; one of the firms surveyed felt it had been forced to an unsuitable location that had higher costs than the site it preferred. Accordingly, there is the risk of building facilities in sites that put a firm at a considerable competitive disadvantage. "It would therefore seem important to ensure that this control is administered by people with relevant experience in the appraisal of industrial projects, and that the appeals procedure is used effectively so that as few firms as possible are left with the belief that their cases have not been considered adequate."[49]

The second generally accepted caveat is that controls will not work consistently under all circumstances.[50] They work only at an optimum in periods of economic growth when many firms are seeking space in which to expand and there are few vacant structures in their vicinity. They are bound to be less forceful during recessions when there is less expansion and facilities are plentiful. Unemployment outside development areas causes pressure to be applied on the government to loosen controls and allow expansion anywhere.

BUSINESS AND LABOR

Any effort to institute a system of locational restrictions to benefit impacted regions would have to consider the attitudes and obtain the cooperation of affected groups, e.g., industry and labor whose firm opposition could prevent or delay initiation of controls. British companies generally prefer to expand in their present locations, whereas, in the United States, industry is more mobile and does not have the same desire to expand in their present sites.

Another contrast is the diversity in viewpoints on IDCs by organized business and labor in Britain. The Confederation of British Industry prefers a long-range policy which encourages improvements to productivity and efficiency rather than locational controls:

> . . . fundamentally it is wrong to use preventative measures in regional policy because they distort those companies who for one reason or another cannot move. On the other hand, regional policy should rely entirely on financial, social and structural improvements. That is a healthy way to go about it. But to deny the development of companies which cannot for one reason or another move into a development area the possibility of expanding or improving their operation is literally to put the brakes on the efficiency of a segment of British industry. [51]

Controls present labor with a dilemma. The IDC is seen in terms of the impact on jobs. The Trades Union Congress follows a policy of avoiding involvement on locational decisions because of trade union bodies in different regions and localities.

> In principle, we have always encouraged Ministers to take a fairly tough line with regard to IDCs to establish priorities such as will help the more heavily unemployed areas as against the others, while recognizing all the while the right of local trade unionists to press their own particular case, as they see fit, in defence of their areas; in much the same way as a Member might in the defence of his constituency. [52]

A REVISED LOCATION POLICY

Inner Cities

After years of denying IDCs for certain inner cities and facilitating movement of industry to assisted areas and new towns, the government in 1977 recognized the desirability of easing controls for inner cities. The severe economic decline of Birmingham and London has been ascribed to particular aspects of the government's dispersal policy. According to Barbara M. D. Smith of the University of Birmingham, the result has been that virtually no new manufacturing activity of any magnitude had taken place since the 1940s. The building of new facilities or the entry of established firms was discouraged and the exodus of industry was encouraged. Therefore, any growth from new products or technology was effectively eliminated and occurred elsewhere. With the expansion of existing enterprises constrained by the IDC requirement, any industrial growth was linked to the prevailing industrial structure and facilities. With deterrents to expansion, diversification or innovation, no replacements emerged for firms that expired, stagnated or moved. [53] The adverse effects of IDCs on Birmingham and London have been compounded by the economic and social forces that have led to the exodus of industry from many aging Western cities even where there are no formal dispersal policies.

For inner cities in the United Kingdom, the relaxation of controls are pertinent primarily to inner London and inner Birmingham. Though Glasgow, Liverpool, Manchester and other large cities are in assisted areas where there is no need for IDCs, they have higher unemployment rates than surrounding environs since regional policy does not distinguish between inner cities and other types of localities within a development area. This demonstrates a shortcoming of the IDC system because inner cities are in development areas, but the impact on employment has been minimal. For example, industry has consistently rejected sites in Glasgow and Liverpool which are in special development areas, and prefer the peripheral and overspill areas which often contain government-sponsored industrial estates and new towns.

The former Labor Government contended that in the nonassisted and intermediate areas, the IDC controls were operated flexibly with due regard to the needs and resources of the areas involved; consequently few IDCs were refused. However, the government made changes, reversing the policy for inner city areas. "What is now required is an intra-regional emphasis to policy designed to help inner areas in the Assisted Areas, and in the non-Assisted Areas."[54] This change in policy was intended to assure that truly mobile projects would be encouraged to consider sites in the assisted areas, but that inner London and inner Birmingham "will in the future take precedence, after the Assisted Areas and in front of the new and expanding towns, in consideration of IDC applications for mobile projects coming forward from the relevant region."[55]

Relaxation of Controls

The Greater London Council (Conservative controlled) sponsored a study, the Marshall Inquiry on Greater London, that recommended the scrapping of office development permits and IDCs since "there is much evidence to show how they have contributed to London's decline."[56] The office development permits were subsequently dropped.

A dim view of relaxing IDC controls was taken by the Town and Country Planning Association, a leading proponent of new towns and decongestion. From a planning viewpoint, IDCs can be valuable in deterring the establishment of large industry in old urban areas. The Association did not favor any easing of IDC control in greater London except for special cases. [57]

A region cannot totally depend on controls to revive its economy; the social and economic infrastructure, external economies, linkages and cost factors have to be taken into account. In the United Kingdom after about thirty years of the IDC system, sharp disparities among and within regions remain. The unemployment rate in parts of London is equal to or higher than in the assisted areas. All of Scotland is still categorized as a development area despite the North Sea oil activity which is enriching parts of the country. In addition, the relevance of IDCs declines when assisted areas encompass over 40 percent of the national work force. There have been periods when IDC policy was strengthened and times when it was weakened. Yet, overall, regional disparities would have been more extreme without IDC controls.

With the return to office of the Conservative Party in 1979, the future of regional policy as it has developed since World War II is uncertain. In view of the changing national and international economic environment, a transition would probably take place regardless of the political party in office. One viewpoint is that "with unemployment nationally over 15 million and inflation over 21 percent, regional policy must now take a subordinate role to industrial problems (such as coping with microtechnology) and inner city policies."[58] The point is not whether regional or locational policy must take a secondary position to industrial policy, but that the two can and must be coordinated to work toward a common goal of economic recovery and growth. [59]

NOTES

1. U. S. , Congress, House of Representatives, Committee on Public Works and Transportation, Subcommittee on Economic Development, Proposals to Extend Economic Development Legislation: Hearings on H. R. 2063 and 3249, 96th Cong. , 1st sess. , 1979, pp. 698-99.

2. "Poor America," Public Interest, no. 60 (Summer 1980): p. 148.

3. "Action on Offices," Business Location File 3, no. 5 (1979): p. 3.

4. Great Britain, Industrial Development Certificates (London: Department of Industry, September 1979), p. 8.

5. Great Britain, House of Commons, Expenditure Committee, Trade and Industry Subcommittee, Regional Development Incentives, Minutes of Evidence from October 1972 to June 1973 and Appendices,

327, Session 1972-73 (London: Her Majesty's Stationery Office, 1973), p. 21 (hereafter cited as Great Britain, House of Commons, 327).

6. Ibid. , p. 22.

7. Great Britain, House of Commons, Expenditure Committee, Trade and Industry Subcommittee, Regional Development Incentives, Minutes of Evidence, July 1973, Appendices and Index, 85-1, Session 1973-74 (London: Her Majesty's Stationery Office, 1973), p. 686 (hereafter cited as Great Britain, House of Commons, 85-1).

8. Great Britain, House of Commons, 327, p. 17.

9. Great Britain, House of Commons, 327, p. 227.

10. Morris L. Sweet and S. George Walters, Mandatory Housing Finance Programs: A Comparative International Analysis (New York: Praeger, 1976), pp. 200-03.

11. Great Britain, House of Commons, 327, p. 230.

12. Great Britain, House of Commons, 327, pp. 79, 82.

13. Great Britain, House of Commons, 327, p. 82.

14. Great Britain, House of Commons, 327, p. 414.

15. Great Britain, House of Commons, 327, p. 93.

16. "Toyota agrees: We'll look at Liverpool," Daily Post (Liverpool), August 19, 1976, p. 1.

17. "Government denies £1M offer to Toyota," Times (London), August 20, 1976, p. 15.

18. "Toyota: It's West Dock or we'll stay put," Evening Post (Bristol), August 19, 1976, p. 1.

19. "Mr. Kawasaki is happy," Economist 268 (July 1, 1978): Survey, p. 13.

20. Quote from Adrian Hamilton, "Inscrutable answers on how to invest that $14 billion," Observer (London), June 25, 1978, p. 15. For a summary of locational policy in Japan see "Locational Controls on Industry: Development Tool for Impacted Regions in Europe and Japan," Urban Innovation Abroad 2 (March 1978): p. 2. For the implications of Japanese manufacturing operations in the United States on domestic industrial relations see Sweet and Walters, Mandatory Housing Finance Programs, pp. 161-62.

21. "No veto: West Dock Pledge," Evening Post (Bristol), August 19, 1976, p. 3.

22. "Toyota: Banned from Bristol," Economist 260 (August 28, 1976), p. 67.

23. "Toyota agrees: We'll look at Liverpool," Daily Post (Liverpool), August 19, 1976, p. 1.

24. "Port 'cheap deal' offer is denied, " Evening Post (Bristol), August 20, 1976, p. 3.

25. "Whitehall's Hara Kari," Daily Telegraph (London), August 20, 1976, p. 14.

26. "Pushing Industry Around," Times (London), August 24, 1976, p. 14.

27. "Varley's Road Block," Daily Telegraph (London), p. 12.

28. Tom Forester, "Regional Policy," New Society 37 (August 26, 1976): p. 49.

29. John Lloyd, "The NEB's pygmy finds a semiconductor jungle," Financial Times, November 8, 1978, p. 22; "Inmos spurns development area," The Observer (London), December 17, 1978, p. 21; "Inmos is about to get more state cash," Economist 274 (February 2, 1980): p. 75; "GEC and Inmos Goodbye Mr. Chips," Economist 274 (May 17, 1980): p. 48; "A stillbirth for Britain's semiconductor industry?," World Business Weekly 3 (July 14, 1980): p. 10; Jane McLoughlin, "Cash for chips in S. Wales: Sir Keith sends 2,000 jobs to area of high unemployment," Guardian (London and Manchester), July 30, 1980, p. 12; and Guy De Jonquieres, "Why Inmos got its £25m. . . " and Alan Cane, " . . . and what it will produce," Financial Times, July 31, 1980, p. 18.

30. "A stillbirth for Britain's semiconductor industry?," World Business Weekly 3 (July 14, 1980): p. 10.

31. See pp. 84-85.

32. Great Britain, Department of Industry, Regional Development Incentives, Government Observations on the Second Report of the House of Commons Expenditure Committee Paper 85, 1973-74, Cmnd. 6058 (London: Her Majesty's Stationery Office, May 1975), p. 11.

33. Great Britain, Secretaries of State for Industry, Scotland and Wales, Annual Report for the year ended March 31, 1979. 206 (London: Her Majesty's Stationery Office, 1979), p. 80.

34. ". . . the decisions of Government on the types and levels of incentives and the application of interdictive controls should be based on as solid a foundation of statistical and other information as possible.

What is most lacking is hard evidence of the effect of regional inducements and IDCs on the decisions of industry." Great Britain, House of Commons, Expenditure Committee, Public Money in the Private Sector, Sixth Report, Vol. I, 347, Session 1971-72 (London: Her Majesty's Stationery Office, 1972), pp. 56-57.

35. John R. Firn, Memorandum in Great Britain, House of Commons, 85-1, p. 695.

36. R. Henderson, "Immigrant industry to Scotland—locational preferences and their relevance to West Central Scotland," in University of Glasgow, Department of Social and Economic Research, Urban and Regional Studies Discussion Paper No. 12, West Central Scotland—Appraisal of Economic Options, III Policies for Employment Growth (July 1973), pp. 17, 19.

37. Gordon C. Cameron and B. Clark, "Industrial Movement and the Regional Problem," cited in R. Henderson, "Immigrant industry," p. 17.

38. A. J. Brown, The Framework of Regional Economics in the United Kingdom, National Institute of Economic and Social Research, Economic and Special Studies 27 (Cambridge: Cambridge University Press, 1972), p. 316.

39. Ibid., p. 318.

40. "The Movement of Manufacturing Industry and the Effect of Regional Policy," Oxford Economic Papers 29 (March 1977): p. 97.

41. "The Effect of Regional Policy on the Movement of Industry in Great Britain," in Duncan MacClennan and John B. Parr, eds., Regional Policy: Past Experience and New Directions (Oxford: Martin Robertson, 1979), p. 61.

42. Barry Moore and John Rhodes, "Evaluating the Effects of a British Regional Policy," Economic Journal 83 (March 1973): p. 90.

43. Ibid.

44. Barry Moore, John Rhodes, and Peter Tyler, "The Impact of Regional Policy in the 1970s," CES Review, no. 1 (July 1977): p. 67.

45. Jim Northcott, Industry in the Development Areas: the experience of firms opening new factories, PEP 43, Broadsheet No. 573, (November 1977).

46. Ibid., p. 63.

47. Ibid., p. 63.

48. Ibid., p. 63.

49. Ibid., p. 63.

50. Ibid., pp. 63-64.

51. Great Britain, House of Commons, 327, p. 387.

52. Great Britain, House of Commons, 327, p. 340.

53. Barbara M. D. Smith, The Inner City Economic Problem: A Framework for Analysis and Local Authority Plans, University of Birmingham, Centre for Urban and Regional Studies, Research Memorandum No. 56 (January 1977), pp. 23-25.

54. Great Britain, Secretary of State for the Environment, Policy for Inner Cities, White Paper presented to Parliament, Cmnd. 6845 (London: Her Majesty's Stationery Office, June 1977), p. 12.

55. Ibid.

56. "Strategic Role for GLC-Marshall," Planning Bulletin, 26/78 (July 14, 1978): p. 100.

57. Town and Country Planning Association, inner cities of tomorrow (London: Town and Country Planning Association, March 1977), p. 10.

58. Jean Hillier, "Barlow's legacy: the demise of regional policy," Planning (Britain), no. 378 (July 25, 1980): p. 7.

59. See chap. 9.

4

CONTROLS IN WESTERN EUROPE

FRANCE

Policy Objectives

The objectives of French regional policy have been to control
the growth of economic activity in the Paris Region thus reducing congestion and diverting mobile projects to the problem regions. A caveat
in considering the application of French regional policy to other countries is that the French government is very concerned with Paris and
its dominance as a primate city. This motivation is without parallel
in major industrialized countries.

The diversion of industry from Paris has been subordinated to
the goal of making Paris a center for the headquarters of national and
international enterprises and is not intended to be at the expense of
the Paris Region.

> The policy of constraint on development in Paris was not
> intended "to sacrifice the future of the capital city and
> that of the provinces," nor to "put Paris based industry
> at the service of regional requirements." It was intended
> as part of a process to implant self-sustaining growth in
> the provincial regions, which would then continue to flour-
> ish independent of either the risk or the timing of further
> decentralizations. Furthermore, it was considered that
> decentralization of jobs from Paris would continue to be
> beneficial to that conurbation. [1]

The Agrément

Major instruments of constraint are licensing, the Agrément, and taxes, the Redevance. An Agrément is a permit or license for the use of additional floor space in the Paris Region. Since the Agrément was initiated in 1955, it has not varied greatly in its legal content but has varied more in terms of implementation. It has the potential for directing moves to specific locations and is implemented through bargaining or package deals. It is unlike the IDC which merely seeks to have firms locate in assisted areas.

An Agrément covers all floor space utilized within the Paris Region; it covers private and public enterprises and institutions, including government installations. An Agrément is required for private firms that have reached their maximum floor space and wish to expand either through new or additional existing floor space when the following limits are exceeded: 1,500 square meters for industrial space; 1,000 square meters for office space; and 5,000 square meters for warehouse space. (A square meter is approximately ten square feet.) There is no exemption limit for the public sector; all expansions, regardless of size, require an Agrément.

Decision Process

Decisions for private sector applications are made by the Ministère de l'Equipment which is the equivalent of the Ministry of the Environment in Britain and the Department of Housing and Urban Development in the United States. For public sector applications, decisions are made by the Comité de Décentralization. Furthermore, the Comité advises the Minister on private sector applications, and its recommendations are mostly the determining factor.

The Comité is composed of representatives from the Délégation à l'Aménagement du Territoire et à l'Action Régionale, the Territorial Planning and Regional Development Agency (DATAR), Paris Prefecture, various ministries, and six individuals nominated by the Prime Minister. DATAR, which is influential, tends to favor decentralization to problem regions. Taking a different view, the representatives of the Paris Region prefer movement to the new towns in the Region over the provinces.

Decisions are generally reached by consensus. From 1975-76, there were differences of opinion within the Comité for about 20 to 25 percent of the applications, but only 5 percent caused delay. [2] An application without problems can be processed within four to six months.

The burden of proof for demonstrating the need for a Paris location rests with the applicant. An appeal can only be made for public sector projects; it is made to the Prime Minister. There is no judicial or administrative appeal procedure for private sector projects, but if there are changes in the application, or compensatory relocations are offered, the firm can reapply. The criteria for approving an application are broad rather than specific.

Projects considered compatible with the employment of "highly qualified" labor in the Paris Region are likely to be approved. The policy began with de Gaulle's wishes to make Paris an international city. Projects considered less important are directed to the provinces.

Factors that are likely to lead to a Paris location are the linkages, national and international activities, headquarters functions, research and development, number and type of jobs, the unsuitability of a location outside of Paris, and compatibility with the physical plan for the Paris Region.

An important feature of the Agrément is bargaining, whereby a project in the Paris Region could be accepted if certain operations are placed in the provinces or problem regions. The small firm unable to decentralize is left at a disadvantage. The bargaining occurs within the context of economie concertée. It is a partnership of big business, the state, and in theory, though not in practice, the trade unions. Positive cooperation rather than conflict is its modus vivendi; "it is fundamentally an attitude of cooperation between the stewards of the state and the managers of big business."[3] The state is the driving force toward economic modernization, increased efficiency, productivity and expansion; the United States is considering similar goals in building an industrial policy but without the same degree of government direction.

The Redevance

The Redevance introduced in 1960 was intended to supplement the Agrément by discouraging new development in the Paris Region through increasing the cost of construction. A tax is applied once to the costs of new industrial and office floor space in the Paris Region with the exception of public sector office space.

For industrial investment, the tax ranges from 0 francs per square meter to 150 francs per square meter; for office floor space, the range is from 0 francs per square meter to 400 francs per square meter. The variations are based on the degree of congestion and the zoning. Firms can thus be encouraged or discouraged in their selection of a location within the Paris Region.[4]

Half of the tax revenues are allocated for infrastructure investment in the Paris Region; the other half is given to a special DATAR fund for infrastructure investment outside the Paris Region to stimulate decentralization.

Since the fee is fixed, inflation has cut the impact of the tax. At their peak the fees are unlikely to be more than 5 to 10 percent of the building costs, and thus not high enough to induce movement out of the Paris Region. [5]

The Redevance fits in with France's long standing role as a pioneer and innovator in fiscal and tax policy. [6] Examples of innovative uses to achieve government policy are the payroll taxes. A tax of 1.7 percent of payroll costs is levied on all establishments with more than nine employees; revenues are allocated to public transit in the Paris Region. [7] A .9 percent tax on payrolls of firms with ten or more employees is utilized for housing. [8]

Effectiveness of Control Measures

How effective have the control measures been with respect to dispersion of industry from Paris and the regeneration of the problem regions? In 1973, the Comité de Décentralization granted approval for construction of over 10 million square feet of industrial space; approval of 21 applications was denied for plants encompassing 1.3 million square feet. From 1960 to 1975, the percentage of approvals to construct industrial buildings of 500 square meters, or approximately 5,350 square feet, in the Paris Region dropped from 26 percent to 8 percent of total construction in France. [9] The number of blue-collar workers (ouvrier) has declined in the city of Paris by 25 percent since 1954, and the number of upper-level managers (cadre supérieur) has increased by 27 percent. [10]

Between 1954 and 1975, approximately 3,150 firms with 460,000 jobs left the Paris Region. [11] The number of jobs is calculated on the basis of jobs relocated plus those immediately created in the new location. The majority, or 57 percent, of the jobs were shifted just a short distance to the Paris Basin; only 35 percent went to partly or fully assisted regions. (See Table 4.1.)

> Even if the assisted areas are not the major recipient of
> relocating jobs, the location of jobs from the Paris Region
> to non-congested, non-assisted areas should be regarded
> as a positive feature even if less desirable than location to
> the assisted areas. [12]

Of major significance in evaluating the control measures is the limited economic benefit to the impacted regions. However, the measures were not designed only to aid such regions; and the growth activities could not be dispersed to the provinces. The Paris Region continues to attract the large capital intensive and high productivity

TABLE 4.1

Decentralization Operations[a] from the Paris Region, 1954-75

Area	Number[b]	Percent
Total	462,210	100.0
Paris Basin[c]	262,800	57.0
Other non assisted areas[d]	39,010	8.0
Partly or fully assisted areas[e]	160,400	35.0

Source: Les Activités, Bulletin d'Information, de la Région Parisienne, No. 21, from Reinhart Wettman et al., Deglomeration Policies in the European Community: A Comparative Study (Berlin: International Institute of Management, 1978), p. 140.

[a]Defined as those operations leaving the Paris Region and decentralizing at least one job. They also relate only to these operations having their headquarters and at least two other establishments in the Paris Region.

[b]Employment figures include both the jobs decentralized and those immediately created in the new location.

[c]Champagne-Ardennes, Picardie, Haute Normandie, Centre, Basse Normandie, and Bourgogne.

[d]Franche-Compté, Rhône-Alpes, Provence-Alpes-Côte d'Azur.

[e]Bretagne, Poitou-Charantes, Aquitaine, Midi-Pyrénées, Limousin, Auvergne, Languedoc-Roussillon, Nord-Pas de Calais, Lorraine, Alsace, and Pays de la Loire.

activities. " . . . Paris is the capital of the most centralized nation in Western Europe. Thus, many businesses not only want to be in the city—they positively need to be if they are to operate efficiently."[13]

> It is clear . . . that the older industrial areas have not benefited greatly by inflows of new jobs, nor is there convincing evidence of indigenous revival.[14]

> . . . the rate of tax in force is unlikely to be sufficiently high to achieve long distance dispersal although the taxes should cause some restructuring of the intra-regional location pattern.[15]

Since 1974, a period of slow growth has ensued, and the effectiveness of the control measures has probably diminished. As a result there has been some concern voiced by the government about the pace of the industrial decline in Paris. [16] The political consensus on the Agrément has been damaged with the emergence of major economic problems nationally, including the Paris Region. "Problems in the donor area obviously reduce the potential of the control to achieve decentralization and reduces the willingness of political representatives of the Paris region to accept controls."[17]

In terms of transferring the major features of the French approach to dispersing industry to the United States, the main obstacle is the lack of a strong national government able to counter the opposition of state and local interests. In addition, a similar consensus or relationship does not exist between U.S. business and government to make bargaining on the location of facilities feasible. Yet, there are potential benefits, and some adaptation could be desirable. The Agrément could be applied to public sector activities, and the Redevance has value in demonstrating how funds could be diverted to areas with infrastructure deficiencies. Instead of indiscriminately granting subsidies to industry, a U.S. tax similar to the Redevance could be placed on construction of facilities while the proceeds are diverted to rebuilding and restoring declining areas. The state and local opposition to initiation and implementation of these changes could be overcome only by a determined Congress.

ITALY

Search for Location Legislation

Prior to the institution of control measures in 1971, for example, the Authorization, regional policy in Italy took the form mainly of incentives and growth center development in the South, and there was little effort to induce movement from the north to the south. In the mid-1960s, plans to effect a control had little success. There were fears, which subsequently were ignored, that firms which were refused permission to expand in the north would move to other European Economic Community (EEC) countries and that administrative problems would be too severe. [18] To establish a north-south linkage, Parliament in the late 1960s passed a resolution seeking government action:

> to introduce some device able to subordinate the granting of requests for permits by medium and large firms to conduct their activities in the North, to the settling on new investments in the South . . . to prevent any measure that could in some way encourage the location of new industrial activity in the congested areas of the country. [19]

The controls that emerged in the form of the Authorization varied considerably from the initial proposals. [20] They applied to private and public industrial investment (but not to the office sector) in the entire country and contained both permit and fiscal elements. Firms not wishing to apply for an Authorization were given the option of paying a tax of 25 percent; or, if the Authorization were denied, they could proceed by paying the tax.

The high exemption limits made the Authorization applicable only to large enterprises. Authorization is necessary for: all new investment over seven billion lire; and any investment, regardless of value, by enterprises listed on stock exchanges; enterprises with capital stock of over five billion lire; and state-controlled firms. In the middle of 1980, the value of the lira was $.001. The value of investment is a more difficult tax measurement for administrative purposes than the size of floor space which was the principal factor with the IDC.

The objective of the control system is to guide the placement of industrial facilities in accordance with the National Development Plan in which the movement of industry from north to south is a key element. Other goals are decongestion of major agglomerations, and intraregional and interregional balance.

Criteria for Approval

Since the Authorization stems from the National Economic Plan (NEP), the criteria for approval have to conform with the Plan. An objective of NEP is a nationally balanced distribution of activity with greatest emphasis on building up the south.

The criteria for an Authorization are not fixed, and allow for a large degree of flexibility in assessing applications. The burden of proof for refusals is on the government; yet the agencies ruling on applications have no framework of regional and economic policies to make their rulings. Statistical data on areas affected by the proposals are lacking.

In practice the decisions tend to be based on the employment impact, physical congestion impact in the proposed site, and the pollution or environmental impact in the area. Mobility potential has not been one of the criteria:

> . . . civil servants have been concerned mainly with evaluating the impact of the new investment on the existing conditions in the area. Indicators concerning the firm's potential mobility have never been considered in the actual implementation of the policy. Only where the investment was

supposed to maintain existing jobs have problems related
to the firm been taken into account . . . in these cases,
there has been a strong argument for granting the Authorization. [21]

The constraining effects of the authorization have been minimal.
Between 1972 and 1975, there were 256 applications: 222 were approved, 27 were automatically granted by not being acted on in three
months, and 7 were refused (4 in the north, and 3 in the south). Of
the 7 companies that were refused an Authorization, none opted to
pay the 25 percent tax and none continued the projects illegally. One
firm modified its application and subsequently received approval for
the desired location in the south. One company abandoned its plans
but this was not fully attributable to the controls; 5 firms appealed
and received approval (3 in the north, and 2 in the south).

The appeals were upheld on the grounds that the government
body exceeded its powers since there was no connection between its
indicators and the goals of the National Economic Plan; there was no
logical connection between the poorly specified territorial objectives
of the Plan and the reasons given for refusal. [22]

The success of the appeals has encouraged firms to apply for
Authorizations and to resist modifying their projects. Also the 25
percent tax on investment costs becomes ineffectual if the courts continue to support their appeals.

Exemption Limits

The exemption limits for the Authorization are set so high that
only large companies have to comply. Yet, an integral part of the
Italian economy is the vast network of small businesses linked to the
giant firms. "This inventive, flexible, and enterprising side of Italian
life, low-cost and labor intensive, coexists in symbiotic profitability
with the economic giants."[23] Paradoxically, the existence of this pro-
fusion of small business, the submerged economy, is not computed
in the official statistics. The province of Naples is reputed to be the
world's largest exporter of leather gloves even though, as the Mayor
of Naples pointed out, "there is not a single glove factory in the
area."[24]

The small entrepreneur is ubiquitous especially in the northern
industrial triangle. The large firm subcontracts to a small workshop
a specific operation that would be too costly to perform in a large
plant. The equipment to perform the operation may come from the
large plant, and the workshop may be owned by an employee of the
large corporation. Goods such as hosiery and shoes are distributed

by the large firms at prices below what it would cost them to produce
the products themselves.

Specialized production centers have arisen, and pressuring the
large firm to relocate facilities could destroy the mutually beneficial
relationships between large and small businesses which are not reflected in the government statistics. It would take an inordinately long
time to build up a comparable relationship. Therefore, controls have
to be applied with sensitivity to avoid destroying these vital linkages.

State enterprises, which have been given an extremely important role in the Italian economy, are subject to the Authorization legislation. The requirement is that 80 percent of new investment and
60 percent of overall investment by state enterprises be in the south.
This requirement is generally interpreted to relate to the total investment that can be placed in the south and not to investments that lack
locational options. [25]

Expectations for Locational Controls

Setting aside the poor state of the national economy, the expected results for the locational controls have not been realized for
a number of reasons: the lack of explicit geographic delineations, the
failure to establish sector priorities, and the absence of clear administrative procedures. [26] The form of the exemption limits, investment
and capital, is more difficult to monitor than floor space or physical
size.

The small number of applications processed is unrealistic and
it would appear that there has been no investment whatsoever from
the leading industrial sectors. Applicants have little fear of the controls because of the successful appeals to the courts. The controls
have demonstrated little or no ability to achieve any significant diversion of industry to the most depressed areas. [27]

The possibility of the tax in its present form becoming a significant control measure appears unlikely. The option of paying the tax
to avoid the application procedure or to overrule refusals gives the
firm the final voice in selecting a location. Though the tax is 25 percent of investment costs, the tax as a proportion of production costs
or selling prices may be much less than 25 percent and thus not
onerous.

The plans for the industrialization of the south, which depend
to a large extent on expansion of state industries, have been jeopard-
ized by the crisis in these industries. Automobiles, chemicals, steel
and telecommunications were among the industries on which the success of these plans was based but the results have been categorized
as Italy's cathedrals in the desert, huge capital intensive projects

which have fallen far short of the expectations. A changed redevelopment policy has diminished the reliance on large-scale projects by seeking to attract investment in and assisting small- and medium-sized enterprises, agriculture (including food processing), and tourism. The stress on small- and medium-sized enterprises, if under the investment limits, would tend to depreciate the importance of the Authorization. [28]

The effectiveness of the controls could be enhanced by trends that could promote the movement of large-scale foreign and domestic investment to the south through diminished business opposition. This movement could occur in conjunction with: the emerging labor shortages in the north where the population has begun to decline; the government policy on purchasing preferences and financial incentives;[29] the proximity to the oil-producing Middle East nations; and the natural shipping outlets, along with the construction of related facilities.

Despite the failure to divert industry sufficiently, the Authorization has several features that may be relevant to U.S. industrial policy: the national coverage and the guiding of government-supported facilities to less-developed areas.

THE NETHERLANDS

Selective Investment Regulation

Before the enactment of the Selective Investment Regulation (SIR) in 1974, prior governments declared that they would not interfere with managements' locational decisions. However, the intensity of the problems in the western part of the Netherlands, and the ripple effect in the remainder of the country caused a reversal of thinking.

The SIR is a mixed system of permits and levies that applies only to the western part of the Netherlands, the Randstad (Rim City). This region contains the largest concentration of population and economic activity, and includes Amsterdam, The Hague, Utrecht and Rotterdam.

Within the Randstad, a permit is required only within the Rijnmond (mouth of the Rhine River) area; in the rest of the Randstad, the government must be notified of proposed projects and has the option of requesting that firms obtain permits.

The intent of the licensing system is to provide the government with an instrument to influence the location of new and expanding establishments. The SIR is concerned primarily with the Randstad and only incidentally with other regions. The goals are to reduce the concentration of activities and population, prevent incursions into the Green Heart or open space section, and achieve an improved and more diversified economic structure. A permit is required for industrial buildings, offices, installations (e. g. refineries), retail establishments, hotels, and restaurants but the SIR does not apply to housing.

Criteria for Approval

The criteria for approval depends totally on the discretion of the government. In general they are the location and size of the building, impact of the building on present and future development. Other factors are the effect on population and housing, extent to which the economic structure is diversified and other activities are stimulated or hindered, and the impact on the current labor market. Mobility criteria are not permitted, i. e. the value of a facility for a problem region cannot be a factor in the decision. As a result, any benefits to problem regions are incidental.

The Rijnmond Public Authority (RPA) has jurisdiction on permits where costs for buildings are between 1 million and 10 million florin and for installations between 5 and 50 million florin. The National Minister of Economic Affairs and Planning gives permits for higher amounts. By mid 1980, a florin or guilder was approximately fifty cents. A distinctive feature of the SIR is that costs, rather than floor space, are the determinant.

A decision on a permit must be made within four months but can be extended for another two months. The applicant can appeal a refusal within thirty days. The burden of proof on refusal rests with the government and not with the applicant.

Between 1975 and 1977, only one of 39 applications for permits was turned down, and one out of 90 in the notification system was refused. [30] The low refusal rate is due to the exemption of alterations or renovations, extensions, and replacements of existing buildings.

The levy was suspended soon after its inception, but has since been reinstituted. The initial levy covered industrial buildings, offices, and installations, with hotels, restaurants, and retail establishments exempt. The new rate is approximately 13 percent for buildings costing over 250,000 florin and 8 percent for fixed outdoor installations in excess of 500,000 florins. The levy is considered part of the cost of the buildings, and thus qualifies as the base when the percentage bonus or incentive to encourage investment is computed. It can also be used for tax depreciation purposes.

SIR has not had a very strong regional impact. A high level of unemployment has made it difficult to reject projects providing jobs. The role of the RPA in approving applications weakens SIR as an effective instrument of national regional policy. There has been very little dispersion of industry to the problem regions. [31] Employers are willing to accept limitations the government opts to impose in the Randstad because the region has a well developed communications and infrastructure, and experienced and reliable labor force. [32]

EUROPEAN ECONOMIC COMMUNITY (COMMON MARKET)

Problem Regions

The efforts of the European Economic Community (EEC) to co-ordinate and rationalize the regional policies of its members should be noted by the United States. These endeavors can serve as guidelines to overcome the probable opposition of individual states and their congressional delegations to any attempts to formulate a strong national regional policy as well as to place limits on financial aids. The European Community (EC) is about one-sixth the size of the United States, but its population of 250 million is larger. The economic and social diversity in the European Community is greater than in the United States, and encompasses a wide range of regional economies from depressed to prosperous.

The problem regions fall into several broad categories that require distinct types of policies tailored to the peculiar problems. The underdeveloped rural regions are overdependent on agriculture, have high levels of emigration, and lack employment opportunities; the infrastructure in these regions is in poor condition or almost nonexistent. Another category is comprised of regions that used to be prosperous but are now in industrial decline. These areas are characterized by high unemployment, emigration, an inability to modernize or replace deteriorating infrastructure, and severe environmental problems. Then there are the congested urban areas or agglomerations with their problem inner cities. A delicate balance has to be maintained in these areas between diverting activity from congested areas and stimulating growth in the inner cities.

Since 1973, the European Community's regional policies have given decongestion equal priority with improvement of the economies of depressed agricultural and industrial regions. One important type of depressed region, areas of urban deprivation, was largely ignored. [33]

> The Commission considers that Community regional policy is not only in the interests of areas of relative poverty, high unemployment and forced migration, but is equally relevant to those living in overcrowded conurbations, with their impoverished environment. The establishment of the Regional Development Fund should not,

therefore, be seen simply as a means of subsidizing the disadvantaged areas by the rich, because in fact it will contribute to the improvement of the environment of the latter.

Efforts to develop the less advanced regions should be accompanied by measures to discourage industrial congestion in areas where saturation already exists, and to achieve decentralization of industrial activity in the general interest . . .

"Regional policy—provided it is rationally deployed . . . is a good investment," as much socially as ecologically and economically. Uncontrolled congestion and migration are more costly than positive intervention to achieve balanced regional development . . .[34]

Proposed Disincentives

In 1977, the Commission proposed to the Council that disincentive measures be studied with regard to their harmonization and coordination since disincentives could become useful to European landuse planning.

> Such measures are already in force in some Member States. However, to be effective both at national and Community level, the limitation sought on economic concentration must be accompanied by expansion in the development and reconversion regions. This cannot happen so long as a firm prevented from investing in one Community region has no difficulty in investing in another similarly congested region of the Community where disincentive measures are not applied.
>
> Disincentive measures coordinated at Community level will, especially in a later period of rising investment, be able to make an effective contribution of human activity throughout the Community in the perspective of European land use planning. [35]

In commenting on the Commission's interest in disincentive measures, the Economic and Social Committee was wary of giving its full support. Disincentives could make a useful contribution to achieving regional policy goals, but cannot by themselves bring about a new distribution of human activity in the Community.

Though the principle of employing disincentives may be

accepted, such measures must lead only to a shift in investment, and not to the complete prevention of investment. The advisability of employing disincentives in periods of low economic activity is very much open to question. Unreserved support of the use of disincentives is not warranted on competition policy grounds alone. [36]

Beyond gathering information on the various member country activities and study, any progress towards instituting a program of disincentives within the Community appears unlikely. "Frankly, given the very low level of investment generally, resulting from the continuing depressed economic situation, it seems politically unlikely that the Member States would accept any extension of controls and disincentives in the near future, but the Commission intends to keep the whole question under constant review. "[37]

The desires of member countries to maintain the integrity of their own programs is tempered by the free capital mobility and customs union in the EEC.

Weaknesses of Disincentives

The proximity of Ireland to the United Kingdom and their strong competition for foreign investment illustrates the gaps or weaknesses in the effectiveness of national disincentives. Both countries are members of the EEC. Yet, Ireland imposes neither controls nor restraints over the corporate selection of locations in either prosperous or depressed regions; thus, Ireland provides an alternative to UK locational controls while competing on the basis of financial incentives. There are no control policies nor any demand for their inception in Ireland. "A country with widespread slack resources has little interest in deterring investment in particular areas. "[38]

Examples of the competition between Ireland and the United Kingdom are the 1963 search by a Ford Motor Company subsidiary for a plant site. Ford considered building a factory in Aycliffe in England, Belfast in Northern Ireland, and Cork and Shannon in Ireland. Belfast was the eventual choice. [39] In 1978, as a result of extremely liberal financial aid, Ford decided to build a 2,500-job factory in Bridgend, Wales rather than in Ireland. [40] The efforts of the Scottish Development Agency to develop an electronics industry in Scotland were undermined by the success in 1979 of the Irish Development Agency "in snatching the American electronics firm Mostek from under the noses of the Scots. "[41]

Harmonizing disincentive policies within the EEC via "Eurocontrol" may have too many obstacles to overcome to be effective. [42]

Countries or regions where there would be an outflow or loss of investment would resist via political measures. There could be an overlap in control between national and EEC authorities. The redistribution of industry would have to be undertaken among regions of extreme differences and of doubtful suitability to accommodate the limited amount of mobile investment in a recessionary world economy.

As part of its competition policy, the Community has taken steps to prevent member states from giving public aid to industries that distort competition and affect trade. Certain social, regional, and sectoral assistance is still allowed. For example, in 1978, there was a ruling against the United Kingdom's Temporary Employment Subsidy because it distorted Community competition policy. As a logical extension of the competition policy, a Community-wide policy on disincentives would appear feasible in a period of economic expansion.

NOTES

1. J. W. House, France: An Applied Geography (London: Methuen, 1978), p. 274.

2. William R. Nicol and Reinhart Wettman, "Background Notes to Restrictive Regional Policy Measures in the European Community," in Kevin Allen, ed. , Balanced National Growth (Lexington, Mass. : Lexington Books, 1979), p. 191.

3. Stephen Cohen, Modern Capitalist Planning (Cambridge, Mass. : Harvard University Press, 1969), p. 52.

4. Reinhart Wettman et al. , Deglomeration Policies in the European Community: A Comparative Study (Berlin: International Institute of Management, 1978), p. 273.

5. Gordon C. Cameron, "Constraining the Growth of Primate Cities: A Study of Methods" in Terence Bendixson, ed. , The Management of Urban Growth (Paris: Organization for Economic Cooperation and Development, Environment Directorate, 1977), p. 155.

6. Morris L. Sweet and S. George Walters, Mandatory Housing Finance Programs: A Comparative International Analysis (New York: Praeger, 1976), p. 32.

7. Cameron, "Primate Cities," p. 154.

8. Sweet and Walters, Mandatory Housing Finance Programs, chap. 3.

9. Jack A. Underhill with Paul Brace and James Rubenstein, French National Urban Policy and the Paris Region New Towns: The Search for Community (Washington: U. S. Department of Housing and Urban Development, Office of International Affairs, April 1980), p. 38.

10. Ibid. , p. 40.

11. Wettman et al. , Deglomeration Policies, p. 28.

12. Wettman et al., Deglomeration Policies, p. 139.

13. "Paris: DATAR restrictions severely limiting new construction," National Real Estate Investor 22 (January 1980): p. 33.

14. Cameron, "Primate Cities," pp. 157, 160.

15. Cameron, "Primate Cities," p. 160.

16. Graham Bentham and Malcolm Moseley, "Socio-Economic Changes and Disparities Within the Paris Agglomeration: Does Paris Have an 'Inner City Problem'?," Regional Studies 14, no. 1 (1980): p. 65.

17. William R. Nicol and Reinhart Wettman, Restrictive Regional Policy Measures in the European Community (Berlin: International Institute of Management, April 1978), p. 46.

18. Kevin Allen and Andrew Stevenson, An Introduction to the Italian Economy (London: Martin Robertson, 1975), p. 202.

19. Nicol and Wettman, Restrictive Regional Policy Measures, pp. 59-60.

20. Nicol and Wettman, Restrictive Regional Policy Measures, pp. 60-63.

21. Nicol and Wettman, Restrictive Regional Policy Measures, p. 4.

22. Wettman et al., Deglomeration Policies, pp. 144-47.

23. "Survey: Italy—Crisis as a way of life," World Business Weekly 3 (May 5, 1980): p. 28.

24. Ibid.

25. Silvio Ronzani, "Background Notes to Regional Incentives in Italy," in Kevin Allen, ed., Balanced National Growth, p. 135 and note 9, p. 153.

26. Ibid., p. 143.

27. Reinhart Wettman et al., Deglomeration Policies in the European Community A Comparative Study: Summary (Berlin: International Institute of Management, n.d.), p. 24.

28. Paul Betts, "The South: The nation's Archilles heel," Financial Times, August 4, 1980, p. 28.

29. "Prospects for Profits: Italy The Next Five Years," Business International 27 (May 9, 1980): p. 151.

30. Wettman, Deglomeration Policies: Summary, p. 24, fn. 1.

31. Wettman, Deglomeration Policies: Summary, p. 24.

32. "Amsterdam: Office space tight, but market is not poised for takeoff," National Real Estate Investor 22 (January 1980): p. 80.

33. "There is an urgent need for some similar system of disincentives [IDCs] to be applied consistently throughout the relatively prosperous regions of the E.E.C. This would not only add some much-needed variety to Community regional instruments, but would also help to prevent the erosion of the effectiveness of disincentive schemes as capital mobility increases within the E.E.C." Reprinted with per-

mission from Regional Studies, 12 (1978), H. W. Armstrong, "Community Regional Policy: A Survey and Critique," p. 518. Copyright, Pergamon Press, Ltd. , 1978.

34. European Communities, European Parliament, Committee on Regional Policy, Regional Planning and Transport, Report on aspects of the Community's regional policy to be developed in the future, Working Document 35/77, April 6, 1977, p. 25.

35. European Communities, Commission, Guidelines for Community Regional Policy: Communications and Proposals from the Commission to the Council, COM 77 195 final, June 7, 1977, p. 11.

36. European Communities, Economic and Social Committee, "Opinion on the guidelines for Community regional policy," prepared September 28, 29, 1977, in Official Journal of the European Communities, 3. 12. 77, no. C292/7, par. 2. 11.

37. Letter, R. J. Jarrett, Commission of the European Communities, Directorate General for Regional Policy, August 8, 1979.

38. James G. Eustace, Regional Problems and Policies in Europe: An Irish Bibliography (Berlin: International Institute of Management, November 1977), IIM/77, p. XIII.

39. Great Britain, House of Commons, Expenditure Committee, Trade and Industry Subcommittee, Regional Development Incentives, Minutes of Evidence from October 1972 to June 1973 and Appendices, 327, Session 1972-73 (London: Her Majesty's Stationery Office, 1973), p. 95.

40. Adam Raphael, "Secret of Ford's extra millions," Observer (London), December 3, 1978, p. 5.

41. Maurice Baggott, "A new thrust for regional development," Director 32 (August 1979): p. 65.

42. Wettman et al. , Deglomeration Policy, pp. 262-65.

5

LOCATIONAL CONTROLS ON FOREIGN DIRECT INVESTMENT

ADOPTION IN THE UNITED STATES

Form of Controls

The location of foreign investment is assuming increasingly importance in international relations and in national economic planning, [1] including regional policies and industrial development. [2] These policies have to be taken into account by corporate planners in making decisions on international operations. [3]

To assure compliance with government policies, the entry of foreign firms into various countries is subject to controls. They vary from indirect methods such as foreign exchange regulations, import and export licenses, using purchases by nationalized industries as a lever, and administrative practices, [4] to direct methods such as approval subject to formal screening processes. [5] The analysis in this chapter covers controls which apply only to foreign firms, and seeks to determine the potential effectiveness of these controls in the placement of foreign-owned facilities in depressed regions. [6]

A distinction should be made between foreign direct investment, the focus of this chapter, and foreign portfolio investment. Direct investment refers to ownership of at least 10 percent of the voting stock, or the equivalent interest, plus a degree of control over the investment. In contrast, portfolio investment implies lack of control over the investment, such as ownership of less than 10 percent of the voting stock or the equivalent interest.

Foreign Investment in the United States

Foreign investment in the United States has been increasing rapidly because of the low value of the dollar, lower costs of production, the large domestic market, less government involvement in the economy, and political and economic stability. (See Table 5.1.) The

TABLE 5.1

Foreign Direct Investment Position in the United States, 1974-78 (Millions of dollars)

	1974	1975	1976	1977	1978*
Netherlands	4,698	5,347	6,255	7,830	9,767
United Kingdom	5,744	6,331	5,802	6,397	7,370
Canada	5,136	5,352	5,907	5,650	6,166
Germany	1,535	1,408	2,097	2,529	3,191
Switzerland	1,949	2,138	2,295	2,651	2,844
Japan	345	591	1,178	1,755	2,688
France	1,139	1,369	1,570	1,800	1,939
Middle East	202	219	201	266	338
All Others	4,396	4,907	5,465	5,716	6,528
Total	25,144	27,662	30,770	34,595	40,831

Source: U.S. Department of Commerce, Bureau of Economic Analysis in U.S. Department of Commerce, International Trade Administration, Office of Foreign Investment in the United States, Canadian Direct Investment in the United States, July 1980, p. 3.
*Preliminary figure.

anticipated continuation of this growth has led to demands that restrictions be placed on acquisitions by foreign firms and that no special treatment be given to such investors. [7] Paralleling these demands is the movement to encourage foreign firms to establish plants in the United States to replace imported goods. [8]

A comparison of regional shares of new foreign-sponsored construction in the United States suggests that the Southeast is increasingly favored by foreign investors as contrasted to acquisitions which tend to go to less prosperous regions such as the Northeast and Middle West. [9] New facilities not only absorb local surplus labor but attract skilled workers from declining regions.

This favorable impact on the creation and location of employment opportunities has been stressed in several studies prepared for the U.S. Department of Housing and Urban Development (HUD). [10] If the United States would create government programs, similar to those in other countries, foreign investment could be managed to create and/or maintain jobs in areas of high unemployment. [11]

SPECIAL TREATMENT

Acquisition or New Investment

Foreign investment merits special treatment because it can bring advanced technology, and growth industries; it stimulates domestic industries through competition, and increases exports. From the standpoint of benefits, a distinction has to be made between acquisitions of existing businesses and the establishment of new businesses. Regional economic benefits from jobs, tax revenues, and the ripple effect are likely to be greater with the establishment of a new business. Whereas with acquisitions, the location of facilities is fixed, at least initially, and any expansion could take place elsewhere. However, the demarcation between benefits from acquisitions versus new businesses is not necessarily clear-cut. An acquisition could mean the survival of an enterprise that would otherwise be liquidated. On the other hand, a new ownership or a takeover could result in streamlining an operation through closing or relocating facilities, and laying off employees. On the whole, however, the establishment of a new operation is more likely to provide the greatest and most immediate return to a regional economy, and thus is the primary focus of this chapter.

In view of the special problems of declining areas, their inability to attract new plants in the face of increasing foreign investment, "Federal and state programs may be needed to stimulate foreign and domestic firms to establish new facilities in such backward or declining areas." [12] A recommended step would be the establishment of boards in the United States, similar to those in Canada and other countries, to review proposals for major investments in acquisitions and new plants.

In the face of the growth of foreign investment, therefore, the U.S. should take advantage of the experience of other industrial host nations as regards policies for the promotion, structuring and regulations of overseas investment in the domestic economy. [13]

A New Federal Policy

Subsequent to these recommendations, the Administration disclosed that, on the initiative of the White House Interagency Coordinating Council, steps would be taken to target foreign investment to economically distressed urban and rural areas that were receiving a declining proportion of foreign investment. The long-standing federal policy of neutrality, neither encouraging nor discouraging foreign investment, would be continued but " . . . it shall be the policy of the Federal government in the future to encourage foreign investors, once they have decided to invest in the United States, to consider locating in distressed urban and rural communities. " 14 (italics in original)

To follow through on this policy, the government intended to take the following steps:

1. Make foreign investors aware of incentives for investing in economically lagging areas.
2. Assist state and local governments in realizing the development potential from foreign investment in distressed areas.
3. Provide research on the job-creating economic development potential of foreign investment. 15

A Congressional committee concluded that the proposed policy and program to entice foreign investment to distressed communities was seriously deficient:

> The new policy changes U. S. policy because, while not the primary purpose, the effect of the Federal activity will be to encourage foreign investment in the United States, irrespective of the type of investment contemplated (i. e. , whether harmful or not), solely on the basis of where it locates.
>
> Because the proposed promotional effort by EDA, HUD, and other agencies, targeted to prospective foreign investors, will be greater than those targeted to domestic investors than would otherwise occur. If this does happen, foreign investors may, in effect, obtain preferential treatment, to the detriment of American investors. 16

An appreciable shift in foreign investment to distressed areas from these initiatives is unlikely. Large foreign firms are well aware of the availability of incentives and the advantages and disadvantages of particular distressed areas. The assistance is more apt to be utilized by small foreign businesses which lack the resources of giant corporations. The programs of foreign countries, which will be examined in this chapter, contain a stronger directional component than the United States steps, and thus could be more effective in placing foreign firms in depressed regions.

FRANCE

Location as a Consideration

Geography has been clearly made a factor in obtaining authorization for foreign direct investment in France, and the government is pressuring foreign companies to create jobs in economically underdeveloped regions. The foreign investment must not endanger sectors the government favors.

The present authorization system grew out of the post-World War II controls on international financial transactions and capital movements. As a means of replenishing the meager foreign exchange reserves, imports of foreign capital were encouraged. One approach was to seek actively all types of foreign investment, particularly from the United States. The government's objective was to coordinate foreign investment with national and regional economic development.

> Investment that would facilitate the expansion of the insufficiently developed segments of the economy, or those undertakings that would contribute to the improvement of France's balance of payments were looked upon with especial favor. [17]

Until 1964, the criteria for foreign direct investment were predominantly economic and financial with less emphasis on the spatial implications of the investment. At the insistence of the newly formed Delegation a l'Amenagement du Territoire et a l'Action Regionale (DATAR), the Territorial Planning and Regional Development Agency, regional economic considerations became crucial in the approval decision. Among Western countries, DATAR is unique in that it is an independent agency, reporting directly to the Prime Minister. DATAR offers foreign entrepreneurs options on alternative sites and can negotiate on location. For example, acquisitions or construction in the Paris area can be sanctioned if other facilities are placed in deprived regions. An aim is to have companies not place facilities in heavily industrialized areas or where they would contribute to even greater dependence on a single industry as opposed to diversification.

The proposed location of the plant site will be considered

in relation to the government's goal of decentralization and creation of new industry in regions of France which have been traditionally underdeveloped and which have not shared in France's current prosperity. [18]

The Review System

Under the regulations embodied in Law No. 66-1008 of December 28, 1966 Relations Financières avec l'Etranger (financial relations with foreign countries) and subsequent decrees and circulars, foreign direct investors are mandated to submit a prior declaration to the government for approval of "the purchase, establishment or expansion of a business concern, a subsidiary or any undertaking of an individual nature: or for a 20% or more equity purchase in a domestic company. A related means of regulating foreign investment is the need to declare and obtain approval of certain transfers of funds to France for purposes of direct investment . . . the establishment of a new enterprise, branch or agency is included."[19] Authorization is not required for investments under $1.2 million. [20]

The French review system is not as highly formal nor as institutionalized as the Canadian. There are no published guidelines or criteria in France. Processing time can vary from six weeks to six months according to the nature and complexity of the project.

The overriding objective of the review is not to reject applications summarily but rather to maximize the domestic benefits by raising the levels of employment, technology, and exports. Concurrently the applicant's needs are not ignored by the imposition of uneconomic demands.

> The authorities have discretionary powers to approve or withhold approval of applications for direct investment. It is, therefore, impossible to list specific criteria determining whether an application will be successful, except the very general criterion that the investment must be of benefit to the French economy. [21]

All investments must be approved by the Comite Interministerial Des Investissements E'Trangers (CIEE) which is presided over by the Minister of Finance. The member agencies do not all have the same priorities and responses. The Minister of Finance is mainly concerned with the balance of payments and the financial ramifications of foreign investment. The Minister of Labor tends to look favorably on investment proposals because of the potential for job creation while weighing shortages or surpluses of labor in the particular region. The Minister of Industry is concerned with the competitive aspects that could seriously impact domestic firms, and DATAR represents the viewpoint that foreign firms could be located in regions needing economic stimulus.

> Rather than viewing foreign investments as categorically good or bad, . . . [government] analyzes the impact which the enterprise would have in important areas of national interest. The process thus is conducive to clear thinking with regard both to the national objectives and to the detail of the investment. [22]

Management Response

The lack of trade and tariff barriers in the Common Market limits the ability to keep a company out of the French market if the approval of foreign investment is denied. A company could set up operations in another member country without fearing that tariffs could be a deterrent.

A firm could accept the suggestion that its preferred location is unacceptable but a change of location could assure favorable action on the application. For example, Motorola proposed building a semi-conductor plant close to the border with Geneva because of the proximity of a national airport and a major university. Prior to granting approval, the Ministry of Finance suggested that the company inspect sites near Lyon, Marseilles, and Toulouse. Although these cities were in a less-developed region, they had the necessary proximity to airports and universities. In March 1966 Motorola selected Toulouse. [23]

Foreign investment can substitute for domestic investment. When the NATO forces were expelled from France and the U. S. military base in Chateauroux was closed, local unemployment increased to a critical level. Numerous French firms refused to build plants in the area. Thus, Alcoa's investment plans in the regions received government approval along with the enthusiastic support of the local populace, especially since United States firms paid higher wages than domestic companies did. [24]

Another example of the regional importance of foreign investment is indicated by the General Motors plans to build a transmission plant in France. The government recommended a location in Strasbourg which gave General Motors proximity to their Opel plant in Germany as well as an ample labor supply. The national economy profited from the increased exports, and the regional economy benefited from losing its traditional reliance on the weak textile industry.

Thus, the location was mutually beneficial to General Motors, and to the national and regional economies. [25]

The screening of foreign investment can also be valuable to the applicants since projects can be evaluated before there are sizable financial commitments. In the case of DATAR, the screening is done by a small cadre of highly skilled professionals. A study of the French policy on foreign investment concludes that the screening could be useful not only in France but in other countries as well.

> Any government which must decide whether a particular investment should be permitted would be aided by analyzing the investment in depth in terms of its impact on specific needs of the country. Of course not all nations' objectives are identical to those of France and, even within a country, needs change over time. Nonetheless the articulation of objectives and the measuring of an investment's impact on those objectives seems a viable method of decision-making. [26]

CANADA

Foreign Investment Review

Any acquisition and control, including small businesses, of Canadian businesses by non-Canadians, and the establishment by non-Canadians of new businesses is subject to review by the Foreign Investment Review Agency (FIRA). The procedure calls for the application to be submitted to FIRA. After review, the application and FIRA's advice are passed on to the Minister of Industry, Trade and Commerce. Provincial authorities also give their views to the Minister who makes recommendations and forwards the application to the Governor in Council, i.e. the Ministry as a whole, which makes the final decision. The primary basis for allowing or refusing the investment is whether it has significant benefit for Canada.

The Foreign Investment Review Act (S.C. 1973-74, c.46 as amended by 1976-77, c.52) became effective in April 1974. The first phase dealt with acquisition of Canadian business enterprises. In October 1975, the second phase covering the establishment of new businesses went into effect. The Act does not apply to the largest growth area, i.e. investment for the domestic expansion of existing operations of foreign-controlled firms.

Initially the intention was to include only takeovers or acquisitions but this raised the likelihood that foreign firms would be encouraged to form new businesses to avoid the review process. Domestic companies would then face strong competition and possibly be driven out of business, whereas through takeover or acquisition, they could sell out at a generous price. [27]

The provincial governments cannot prevent the Canadian government from approving a proposal; however, it is unlikely that there would be any attempt to overrule provincial disapproval since their views carry considerable weight. It is estimated that provincial governments disagree with about 2 percent of FIRA's recommendations[28] since ". . . good and effective working relations have developed between the Agency and provincial departments and significant differences of view are indeed few and far between."[29] Provincial governments have to consider the potential for intraprovincial conflicts among local governments when reviewing a proposal.

The approval rate for all applications has been approximately 85 percent. (See Table 5.2.) The approval rate could vary if the applications withdrawn while under review were excluded; the withdrawals could indicate anticipation of disapproval or a reversal in the initial decision to invest. The FIRA has been criticized for being too lax in allowing so many proposals to proceed and the new 1980 Trudeau Cabinet included a strong proponent of this viewpoint. With unemployment at a high level, other ministers were unlikely to concur with any discouragement of investments that would create jobs; another Cabinet split reflected two views: working to funnel investment to depressed regions vs. discontinuing the sheltering of inefficient industries from foreign investment. [30]

TABLE 5.2

Canada—Disposition of Applications for Investment to Foreign Investment Review Agency, April 9, 1974 to March 31, 1979

	Acquisitions		New Business		All Applications	
	Number	Per-cent	Number	Per-cent	Number	Per cent
Disposition	1038	100.0	872	100.0	1910	100.0
Allowed	863	83.1	750	86.0	1613	84.5
Disallowed	90	8.7	46	5.3	136	7.1
Withdrawn during review	85	8.2	76	8.7	161	8.4

Source: Government of Canada, Foreign Investment Review Agency, ANNUAL REPORT 1978-79 (Ottawa: October 1979), p. 29.

Location as a Factor

There is no explicit mandate for industries to locate in depressed regions though location is discussed before a firm's application is approved. The Grey Report, which was instrumental in the establishment of FIRA, stated that the review process could facilitate the government's desire to improve economic conditions in the slow-growth regions. The review agency could be directed to consider location in a slow-growth region as a positive benefit when assessing the net impact of the investment on Canada. [31] However, the government was reluctant to intervene too directly in the sensitive issue of location. While a takeover involves only existing facilities, new investment calls for determining where new plants should be located, an issue of utmost importance to provincial political figures avid to bring jobs to their constituents. [32] Location is still a consideration; both the federal and provincial governments want to bring new foreign capital to depressed regions.

The key provision of the Foreign Investment Review Act is Subsection 2(2) which lists the factors to be taken into account when evaluating whether an investment meets the test of significant benefit to Canada. Significant benefit has never been sufficiently defined to satisfy the business community. The factors are:

1. The effect on the level and nature of economic activity in Canada, including the effect on employment, resource processing, exports, and the utilization of Canadian parts, components, and services;
2. The degree and significance of participation by Canadians in the business enterprise and in the industrial sector to which the enterprise belongs;
3. The effect on productivity, industrial efficiency, technological development, innovation, and product variety;
4. The effect on competition within any industry or industries in Canada;
5. Compatibility with national industrial and economic policies, taking into consideration industrial and economic policy objectives enunciated by the federal government and any province likely to be significantly affected by the proposed investment.

The relative significance given to each factor is not the same for all transactions. It varies with the nature of the transaction, the industry, and the region; for example:

. . . an increase in economic activity in a slow growth area may be judged to be more beneficial than in an area whose resources are already virtually fully occupied . . .

increases in efficiency or competition are given greater weight if they are expected to occur in industries where such changes are likely to have a far reaching impact on economic performance. [33]

Adoption by the United States

Regarding its applicability to the United States, FIRA is a model of a program through which foreign investment could be directed to specific locations in response to domestic economic needs. After studying FIRA, the General Accounting Office concluded that this type of agency was not suitable for the United States, but there was no consideration in the report of location as a factor in foreign direct investment. [34] A Congressional committee studying foreign investment in the United States disagreed with the General Accounting Office. The committee recommended that Congress favorably consider proposals for a screening agency. The Cohen Report, prepared for HUD, recommended that serious consideration be given to the establishment of a national board along the lines of FIRA. [35]

The review mechanism gives government a flexibility in that investment proposals can be considered on an individual basis; therefore, approvals can be granted in conformity with the prevailing economic strategy or industrial policy. However, extremely sharp fluctuations in granting approvals can be disturbing to business by hindering planning and thus delaying or deterring the implementation of business decisions.

The smooth-working relationship between the federal and provincial governments on foreign investment could be difficult to replicate in the United States; on many issues it is not without conflict in Canada. The individual states have developed too strong an independent role in terms of competitive industrial development policies and programs to accept willingly any diminution of their authority. A preliminary step to pave the way for the institution of a review process in the United States would be an attempt to limit the fierce interstate competition for industry. [36]

AUSTRALIA

In Australia, business takeovers are subject to review and approval under the Foreign Takeovers Act of 1976. Foreign investment transactions not covered by the statute, notably the establishment of new businesses, are screened through voluntary compliance. The voluntary compliance is backed up by foreign exchange and export controls; refusal to submit to the screening process could bring a denial of foreign exchange and export permits.

An investment proposal is examined to determine whether it will produce directly or indirectly net economic benefits to Australia with respect to a particular industry along the following lines:

1. Competition, price levels, and efficiency;
2. The introduction of technology, or managerial, or work force skills new to Australia;
3. The improvement of the industrial or commercial structure of the economy, or of the quality and variety of goods and services available in Australia;
4. The development of, or access to, new export markets.

If the proposal is deemed not to be detrimental to the national interest on the basis of the above standards, the following criteria are then applied:

TABLE 5. 3

Australia—Disposition of Applications for Screening, 27 months ending June 30, 1978

	Cases		Assets or Investment Percent
	Number	Percent	Percent
Disposition	2123	100. 0	100. 0
Allowed	2107	99. 2	98. 9
Acquisitions of control	524	24. 7	30. 0
Examinable change of ownership	883	41. 5	n/a
Acquisitions of real estate	622	29. 3	4. 5
New businesses	78	3. 7	64. 4
Disallowed	16	. 8	1. 1
Acquisitions of control			
Examinable change of ownership	8	. 4	. 2
Acquisitions of real estate	1	. 1	n/a
New businesses	7	. 3	. 9

Source: Government of Canada, Foreign Investment Review Agency, A comparison of foreign investment controls in Canada and Australia, FIRA Papers No. 5 (Ottawa: April 1979), p. 16.

TABLE 5.4

Australia—Sector Distribution of Screened Investments,
27 months ending June 30, 1978

| | Cases | | Assets |
	Number	Percent	Percent
Sector distribution			
Acquisitions of control	524	100.0	100.0
Agriculture	96	18.3	2.1
Mining, oil and gas	34	6.5	30.5
Manufacturing	146	27.9	15.1
Other	248	47.3	52.3
			Investment Percent
New businesses	81	100.0	100.0
Agriculture	2	2.5	.1
Mining, oil and gas	22	27.2	78.4
Manufacturing	13	16.0	16.5
Other	44	54.3	5.0

Source: Government of Canada, Foreign Investment Review Agency, A comparison of foreign investment controls in Canada and Australia, FIRA Papers No. 5 (Ottawa: April 1979), p. 17.

1. Whether the business concerned could subsequently be expected to pursue practices consistent with the country's best interests:
   A. Local processing of materials and utilization of domestic components and services;
   B. Involvement of Australians on policy-making boards of businesses;
   C. Research and development;
   D. Royalty, licensing, and patent arrangements;
   E. Industrial relations and employment opportunities;
2. Whether the proposal would conform with other government economic and industrial policies;
3. The extent to which Australian equity participation has been sought and the level of Australian management subsequent to implementation of the proposal;
4. Taxation considerations;
5. The interests of Australian shareholders, creditors and policy holders affected by the proposal. [37]

The decision on approval is made by the Treasurer on the advice of the Foreign Investment Review Board. The screening process does not ordinarily include consultation with state authorities; however, for some major investment proposals, discussions are held with the appropriate state authorities.

The large number of transactions screened is due to the inclusion of real estate and transfers of share ownership not involving shifts in control. Only a small proportion of investment or number of transactions, about 1 percent, are denied. (See Table 5. 3.) Locational factors are not explicitly included in the aforementioned criteria, possibly because in the natural resource sector, which constitutes almost 80 percent of new business investment, choice of location is not a viable option. (See Table 5. 4.) Though Australia's screening does not heavily involve location, it is compatible with the growing interest in the United States in industrial policy. [38]

SWEDEN

Domestic Business Support for Controls

The general public might believe that domestic businesses are likely to be indifferent to proposals for controls on foreign businesses; however, the attitude of the leading Swedish business organizations belies this theory and indicates that the indifference of domestic business toward controls cannot be taken for granted.

Proposed legislation would give the government the power to control products, investment, research spending, and employment levels of all foreign-based companies. [39] The government appointed a committee, representing diverse interests, to study the legislation. The members disagreed on the extent to which foreign direct investment merited "social control of the establishment and the activities of foreign-owned companies. " But there was agreement that foreign direct investment can bring the country such advantages as "capital, jobs, export opportunities and new knowledge as regards technology, marketing and business management and that in these and other ways foreign direct investments, may promote the differentiation, efficiency and international competitiveness of the Swedish economy. "[40]

Within the committee three preliminary drafts were prepared, yet none received majority support. The draft supported by Social-Democrats and trade unionists called for controls within the framework of a concessions system; foreign-owned companies would undertake business activities only by special permission conditioned on assurances that they would not be in contravention of the public interest, i. e. observance of the OECD guidelines for multinationals. New conditions could be attached to the concessions and the old ones revised. There would also be controls over takeovers.

The center and liberal groups also called for controls on the establishment of foreign businesses, and sought solutions through negotiation to concrete problems arising from the activities of foreign-owned companies. Permission would be required only for the establishment of new enterprises. There would be controls on takeovers and negotiations if the company did not adhere to internationally accepted guidelines for multinational enterprises or if a danger to the public interest arose.

The draft supported by the Conservatives and industry approved some limitations on foreign takeovers in accordance with the OECD code on liberalization of capital movements. However, the activities of foreign-owned companies should not be controlled by any other means than those applied to Swedish industry.

Retaliatory Measures

The leading business organizations, Federation of Swedish Industries, Confederation of Swedish Employers, Swedish Importers and Wholesalers Association, and Swedish Federation of Crafts and Industries, jointly opposed the regulations on the grounds that "the ultimate right to make vital business management decisions is taken away from companies and given to public agencies which bear no economic responsibility for the expenses of these [foreign] companies."[41] Furthermore, discriminatory measures against foreign companies could result in international countermeasures against Swedish foreign investments; exports could also suffer from retaliatory action. Swedish business is particularly vulnerable because of its heavy dependence on income from foreign trade and investment.

> The companies affected regard the proposals contained in the control and negotiation alternatives as a major change for the worse in investment conditions for foreign companies in Sweden. The first likely effect will presumably be that the establishing of new operations by foreign companies—which is already at far too low a level will be drastically affected. Already established companies will presumably be mainly discouraged from making long term investments, not least those investments which involve research and development commitments.[42]

The opposition of Swedish business is an indication of what might be expected from the segment of United States business heavily reliant on foreign trade. The extreme dependence of the Swedish economy on foreign activity is not comparable in the United States. Foreign business is more attracted to investment in the United States, e. g. the size of the domestic market, and therefore would be more willing to accept controls without taking countermeasures against U. S. business.

JAPAN

Discouragement of Foreign Investment

Japan has long feared that outsiders would dominate its major industrial sectors; therefore, the ability to invest in that country has been subject to restraints designed to limit the role of foreigners in the domestic economy. Except for the immediate post-World War II period, when Japan sought foreign investment as a source of capital and technology, foreign investment has been actively discouraged. By 1979, the government reluctantly acknowledged that the stringent constraints had to be relaxed. Steps were taken to liberalize the investment process, although investment was not necessarily directed to depressed regional economies.

> At present there is recognition that if Japanese industry
> is to be permitted to invest abroad, reciprocity is neces-
> sary. Liberalization of current government policies which
> directly impact on foreign investment is in process, as is
> liberalization of a variety of other policies which indirectly
> affect the operations for foreign—or United States—invested
> manufacturing operations. To what extent policies are ac-
> tually liberalized, however, will in large measure depend
> on the way in which new laws and regulations, when they
> are issued, will be administered. [43]

After World War II, the control of internal foreign investment started in 1951 with the Law Concerning Foreign Investment; the intention was to protect Japanese-owned firms from foreign competition. To rebuild Japanese economic power and to maintain the American strategic military position in the Pacific, the United States tolerated Japanese restrictions on direct investment and the barriers to U. S. exports. As the security concerns of the United States in the Pacific eventually receded, the complaints of U. S. corporations against Japanese investment and trade policies were increasingly taken into account by U. S. officials. [44]

Japan's primary regulatory device was to delay resolving the case-by-case screening process. Sometimes hints were given by government sources or the involved Japanese private interests. If foreigners responded appropriately to the signals, approval was forthcoming. [45] From the standpoint of the host government, case-by-case screening gives the host government a means of directing foreign firms to critical locations; however, ". . . it is important that restrictions be based on explicit laws as much as possible so that the impartiality of the policy and of its implementation can be clearly seen in both host and investing countries. "[46]

A Liberalized Policy

In 1963 and 1964, Japan by virtue of its membership in the International Monetary Fund and the Organization for Economic Cooperation and Development had to liberalize its policies on direct foreign investment. The result was that in July 1967 the case-by-case screening of all inward investment was replaced by the "positive list" formula which specified a number of industrial sectors where 100 percent foreign ownership was permitted (first category), and industrial sectors where foreign capital participation up to 40 percent was permitted (second category). In 1971, there was a shift to a negative formula, which was free in principle and exceptions were listed. In 1976, the exceptions for 100 percent ownership were confined to four industries: agriculture; forestry and fishing; mining and oil; and leather manufacturing. Other sectors allowing less than 100 percent ownership were also specified.

In December 1979, sweeping changes in foreign investment and exchange laws that removed restrictions were approved by Parliament. However, controls could be imposed in emergency periods. [47]

A supposedly simple procedure for requiring prior notification of inward investment was instituted. Only investments in the four industries specified in 1976, or in businesses that would have an extremely adverse effect on domestic industries were excluded. [48]

The revised Foreign Exchange and Foreign Trade Control Law states that, after giving advance notice to the Minister of Finance, the minister or ministers having jurisdiction over the enterprise can change or suspend, within a fixed period, the nature or content of the direct investment if the investment:

1. Would impair security of the nation, public order or public safety;
2. Would have adverse effects on the activities of the same kind of domestic enterprise or smooth operation of the national economy;
3. Is from a foreign country with whom there is no reciprocity;
4. Is equivalent to the amount of capital transactions for which permission is required. [49]

The Outlook for Direct Foreign Investment

Whether there will be any appreciable difference from the positive list formula remains to be seen; the high entry costs could render the changes meaningless. [50] The requirement for discussions with the Ministry of International Trade and Industry before a corporate investment plan can be concluded is critical in terms of location. [51] Foreign firms have not yet attained the desired degree of flexibility for investment. "It is a very long and arduous process to establish a 100 percent owned subsidiary in Japan. "[52]

The obstacles to entering Japan via direct investment are so numerous and complex that location does not become a matter of great consequence.

> . . . the high costs of entry to Japan-acquiring land, warehouses and plant, searching out staff in a country with little job mobility, building a distribution system, establishing a brand position—all must be expenses out of current earnings. And with dollar devaluation, the already high cost is rising rapidly to even higher levels. Few United States companies and few United States managers are in a position to undertake that sort of reduction in reported earnings for the sustained period necessary to establish a position in a highly competitive market [53]

It is difficult to envision the Japanese system of restraints on foreign investment being adopted in the United States which has a more open economy and liberal acceptance of foreign investment. This Japanese industrial strategy is too contrary to the American tradition to be accepted even in a modified form.

INSTITUTING CONTROLS IN THE UNITED STATES

Foreign Direct Investment Policy

How feasible is a shift in the U. S. policy on foreign direct investment from one largely free from special regulation to one which strongly advocates channeling new foreign-owned facilities into depressed regions? What form should the directives take? What would be the reaction of domestic and foreign enterprises, and state and local interests to the imposition of restraints? While a limited number of regional economies might benefit, would there be a net loss to the national economy if investment is lost to other countries because of opposition to the controls?

Presently there is no organized or formal plan by the federal government to direct foreign investment in facilities to economically impacted regions. The aforementioned process whereby the federal government discusses with foreign investors the availability of sites in depressed regions is an important step toward achieving this goal.

A more positive step would be a process of stronger persuasion or negotiation modeled after the French review system which does not stipulate specific prerequisites for approval. Each proposal would be considered in the light of regional development needs and national economic conditions at the particular period while not overlooking the investor's special circumstances.

A problem with case-by-case screening is that it may not be compatible with corporate planning. Before submitting an application, a firm has already made a commitment in the form of expenditures on preparing development plans and evaluating sites. Administrative latitude and subsequent changes in the rules because of new political alignments may be less desirable than having to comply in advance with known and specific guidelines. A degree of uncertainty is eliminated by the United Kingdom industrial development certificate system which requires review only for locations outside of the assisted areas.

How would domestic firms react to the institution of a system of restraints applicable only to new foreign investment? The response could range from indifference to strong opposition, e. g. Sweden. There could be concern over the possibility that the controls could eventually be extended to cover all firms, domestic as well as foreign. Strong opposition would result from the denial of new foreign investment if the business generated by the new foreign facilities represents an addition to the profits of domestic firms, either as suppliers or distributors. This opposition need not necessarily be regional in scope. Another category consists of the segment of the business community that opposes controls in general on philosophical or ideological grounds.

Foreign firms are not always adamantly opposed to locating in depressed areas[54] and will usually not seek to dispute the wishes of host governments if the criteria are reasonable. There are advantages to be gained by multinationals from locating in depressed areas. International corporations are subject to severe criticism for having too much economic power, for lacking social responsiveness, and for being indifferent to domestic problems. This criticism can be countered by placing facilities in depressed regions, gaining support and goodwill in the region, and achieving political support from regional interests at the national level.

If foreign entrepreneurs are dissatisfied with decisions, they do not lack countermeasures. When the economy is in a downturn, they have increased bargaining power and are less willing to accept suggestions for locations that are not their first choice. As tariffs are lowered and depending upon transportation costs, they have the option or means of penetrating a national market from another country.

The impact of controls on multinationals can be avoided through a shift from traditional forms of equity investment and direct management control to "unbundling" the investment package. These firms can sell management and marketing services, technology of license technology, and need not own facilities. Therefore, the multinational firm has no concern over where facilities are placed as long as there is no significant diminution in revenues because of an uneconomic location.[54]

NATIONAL VS. SUBNATIONAL INTERESTS

At the subnational level, the imposition of central government controls on foreign investment would not be accepted with equanimity. The reason is that preference might be given to national over subnational concerns since the national government could limit location to depressed areas. The national government's concerns with foreign investment could be focused on foreign policy, balance of trade, and exchange controls at the expense of local economic development or subnational interests. Local interests would be only one of the factors taken into account in deciding whether to permit the foreign investment.

> A central government may be willing to run the risk that a foreign investment will not take place by bargaining for better terms and conditions, or may deliberately prevent it from taking place by acting in terms of a principle of economic nationalism. The central government can do this because the particular foreign investment appears relatively unimportant when measured on the scale of the whole national economy. For a provincial or state government, on the other hand, a particular proposed investment in the province or state may loom very large, and may even appear as the key to the province's or state's economic prospects. [56]

The political structure of the United States does not readily lend itself to strong regulations on foreign investment. A federal structure entails "the presence of regional governments with claims to elected political legitimacy equal to that of the central government—to actively argue the regional and to some extent other group differences that exist in any state. The jurisdiction of such regional governments includes varying degrees of capacity to use their own policies to challenge the decisions of the central government in balancing competing domestic interests. Thus, in decentralized federal systems . . . there are important consequences and some important constraints to take into account in considering policies regarding multinational enterprises."[57]

Even the United Kingdom, which has a stronger central government than the United States, has difficulties in favoring depressed areas when recruiting foreign firms. The primary agency responsible for attracting foreign investment to the United Kingdom is the Invest in Britain Bureau of the Department of Industry. An example of criticism of this policy comes from a nonassisted area by the industrial development adviser of the Warwickshire County Council:

> Now I recognize the difficulties the Assisted Areas face, and understand the argument for fiscal measures to alleviate them but are non assisted areas themselves really so prosperous and inundated with investment from both elsewhere in the U. K. and abroad—that no promotional efforts are needed? Can the U. K. really afford to present a national image comprised almost solely of those parts of the country that are, by definition, less than optimum areas for industrial location?"[58]

Strong opposition to controls favoring particular areas would come from state and local interests engaged in the heated rivalry to attract industry. The rivalry is extended to Congressional concern for their constituencies and is reflected in the generous subsidies available in both prosperous and depressed regions. The accelerating competition through liberal subsidies has reached a point where they cancel each other out and many grantors would be pleased to see them discontinued. [59] A review process could be a means of circumscribing the granting of excessive subsidies to foreign firms that do not locate in designated areas.

LIMITING SUBSIDIES

Supranational Restrictions

Some limits have been placed on the subsidies that attract industry from other countries. Through its competition policy, the European Economic Community restricts subsidies to the extent that the subsidies compensate for the added costs of conducting business in depressed regions. The United States is a signatory of the Multilateral

Trade Negotiations of the General Agreement on Tariffs and Trade which looks unfavorably on nontariff barriers in the form of subsidies. Subsidies to attract industry that demonstrably injure other countries or foreign industries by lowering the costs of exports must not be used.

Efforts to limit the state and local financial inducements in the United States to foreign investors have been led by C. Fred Bergsten, Assistant Secretary of the Treasury for International Affairs. [60] The practicality of this kind of move is questioned by Walter Evans, a Washington, D. C. lawyer. His viewpoint could also be applied to locational controls:

> If federal officials try to restrict state and local govern-
> ment efforts to attract foreign investment, they are going
> to run into a hornets' nest. It's hard to imagine a member
> of Congress voting against programs designed to attract
> new jobs to his or her state. And that's how the issue will
> be portrayed. [61]

Subsidies and Locational Controls

An objective of the review process could be to circumscribe, in tandem with locational controls, the granting of subsidies that attract industry to thriving regions. The review process could, in turn, enhance the desirability of sites in depressed regions. One proposal calls for foreign recipients of national, state, and local financial aids to remain committed to declining areas:

> Regulations would be needed to assure the long term com-
> mitment of industry to such places [declining areas] if fed-
> eral program subsidies or local funds are utilized by for-
> eign investors in making the initial investments. This could
> be done through clauses in industrial bonds and other financ-
> ing arrangements which are used to attract such investors
> or through national, state or urban industrial regulations. [62]

A first step has been taken by the federal government, i. e. to formulate a process for discussions with foreign companies concerning the likelihood of voluntarily locating in depressed areas. The precedents exist for instituting stronger measures without destroying the attractiveness of the United States for foreign investors. [63] The experience of other Western democracies, notably Canada and France, reveals that direct controls could be established and function with the acquiescence of foreign enterprises and without the violation of international codes of conduct.

The key point in imposing any limiting measures is that the potential for profit should not be harmed. Controls and profitability are not necessarily diametrically opposed. With guidelines sensitively applied, there need not be a diminution of the significant contribution foreign investment can make to revitalizing the economy at the sectoral and regional levels.

NOTES

1. ". . . we see an increasing trend away from concern about the ownership and control of productive facilities toward greater concern about their location. For the developing world, this has translated into calls for redeployment of production facilities to the poorer countries. In the developed world, following the most serious recession since the great depression, it is a question of the preservation and growth of employment opportunities. The conflict embodied in these inconsistent goals will be an important factor in intergovernmental relations on investment issues in the near term." Julius L. Katz, "International Direct Investment," in Private Investors Abroad—Problems and Solutions in International Business, Southwestern Legal Foundation (New York: Matthew Bender, 1977), pp. 181-182.

2. "Incentives and disincentive measures are used by [OECD] member governments to influence the nature, location and size of [international] direct investment for a variety of policy purposes such as industrial, regional, technology, employment and trade policies. Often these incentive and disincentive measures are part of the overall economic policies of member countries." Organization for Economic Cooperation and Development, International Investment and Multinational Enterprises: Review of the 1976 Declaration and Decisions (Paris: 1979), p. 55.

3. Albert H. Jaeggin, "One World Concept in Facility Planning Becomes a Reality," Area Development 14 (December 1979): p. 4.

4. "This [administrative practices] is an area where transparency is inherently difficult, but it is also one of particular importance to the question of National Treatment. It is believed that discrimination through seemingly arbitrary decisions or prolonged delays is often more burdensome to the foreign-controlled enterprises than restrictive laws or regulations which are known and predictable." Organization for Economic Cooperation and Development, National Treatment for Foreign Controlled Enterprises Established in OECD Countries (Paris: 1978), p. 6.

5. "Perhaps the single most common instrument which other countries use in dealing with foreign direct investment is some form or other of review of screening mechanism. In some countries, it is

used very infrequently as an instrument of intervention. In other cases the screening mechanism is used more often—either to restrict or to bargain, or both. The review mechanism provides a national government with flexibility to consider foreign direct investment on a case by basis and the vigor with which a review process is applied can be made to vary over time." Government of Canada, Foreign Direct Investment in Canada (Ottawa: Information Canada, 1972), p. 336.

6. "To combat American multinationals, they [Europeans] force foreign investors to take domestic firms as partners, to share technologies, and to invest in depressed regions." Douglas F. Lamont, Foreign State Enterprises: A Threat to American Business (New York: Basic Books, 1979), p. 28.

7. "Prospects for Profits: The United States," Business International 26 (September 7, 1979): p. 284.

8. To offset the effects on sales of U.S.-produced autos from increasing imports of Japanese cars, the U.S. government, with strong trade union and steel industry support, was attempting early in 1980 to persuade Japanese auto manufacturers to move part of their production to the U.S.; otherwise, import restrictions could be imposed. To ease trade friction, the Japanese government was urging these companies to limit the number of cars shipped; and as had been done with television sets, Japan would set up plants in the U.S. The issue of locating the plants in depressed areas had not yet arisen.

9. Jane S. Little, "Locational Decisions of Foreign Direct Investors in the United States," New England Economic Review (July/August 1978): p. 53.

10. Gage B. A. Haskins, The Impact of International Trade and Investment Policy: A Policy Briefing Paper, prepared for the U.S. Department of Housing and Urban Development (Washington: Fry Consultants, November 1977); and Robert B. Cohen, The Impact of Foreign Direct Investment on United States Cities and Regions, prepared for the U.S. Department of Housing and Urban Development under Contract 5193 79 (Arlington, Va.: The Analytic Sciences Corporation, February 1979).

11. Haskins, International Trade, p. 23.

12. Cohen, Foreign Direct Investment, p. 9-2.

13. Ibid., p. 9-8.

14. U.S., Departments of Commerce and Housing and Urban Development, Federal Policy Towards Foreign Direct Investment in Distressed Areas, May 19, 1980, p. 3.

15. United States Department of Commerce News G80-95, Office of the Secretary, "White House Initiative Aims at Targeting Foreign Investments to Economically Lagging Areas," May 19, 1980, p. 2.

16. U.S., Congress, House, Committee on Government Operations, The Adequacy of the Federal Response to Foreign Investment

in the United States: Twentieth Report, 96th Cong., 2d sess., August 1, 1980. H. Rept. 96–1216, p. 45.

17. Allen J. Johnstone, United States Direct Investment in France (Cambridge, Mass.: MIT Press, 1965), p. 24.

18. Charles Torem and William Laurence Craig, "Control of Foreign Investment in France," Michigan Law Review 66 (February 1968): p. 700.

19. Government of France, Delegation A L'Amenagement du Territoire et A L'Action Regionale, Investment and Export Financing (November 1977), pp. 4–5.

20. "France Relaxes Rules On Direct Investment By Foreign Companies," Wall Street Journal, August 12, 1980, p. 31.

21. "In fact, all investment decisions are made on a strictly case-by-case basis, said a finance ministry official." Felix Kessler, "France's Erratic Policies on Investments By Foreigners Confuse Many U.S. Firms," Wall Street Journal, April 7, 1980, pp. 6, 24.

22. Robert B. Dickie, Foreign Investment: France A Case Study (Leyden, Netherlands: A. W. Sijthoff; and Dobbs Ferry, N.Y.: Oceana Publications, 1970), p. 94.

23. Ibid., p. 86.

24. Ibid., p. 86.

25. Ibid., p. 87.

26. Ibid., pp. 94–95.

27. John Fayerweather, Foreign Investment in Canada: Prospects for National Policy (White Plains, N.Y.: International Arts and Sciences Press, 1973), p. 147.

28. U.S., Comptroller General to Hon. Benjamin S. Rosenthal, Chairman, Subcommittee on Commerce, Consumer, and Monetary Affairs, House of Representatives, Should Canada's screening practices for foreign investment be used by the United States?, ID–79–45 (September 6, 1979), p. 4.

29. Gorse Howarth, "Personal notes on the review process," Foreign Investment Review 1 (Autumn 1977): p. 10.

30. "Canadian nationalism again threatens MNCs: A foe of foreign investment will press his views," World Business Weekly 3 (April 7, 1980): pp. 6–7; and "Constraints in Canada May Work Against Trudeau's Stance on MNCs," Business International 27 (July 18, 1980): p. 229.

31. Government of Canada, Foreign Direct Investment in Canada (Ottawa: Information Canada, 1972), p. 457.

32. Fayerweather, Foreign Investment, p. 148.

33. Government of Canada, Foreign Investment Review Agency, Foreign Investment Review Act: Annual Report 1977/78 (Ottawa: October 1978), p. 55.

34. U.S., Comptroller General, Canada's screening practices.

35. U.S., Congress, House, Committee on Government Opera-

tions, Response to Foreign Investment pp. 55, 162; and Cohen, Foreign Direct Investment, pp. 9-5, 9-8.

36. Barney Frank, "Sorry States: Federalism as a protection racket," New Republic 181 (December 29, 1977): p. 7; and Robert Goodman, The Last Entrepreneurs: America's Regional Wars for Jobs and Dollars (New York: Simon and Schuster, 1979).

37. Government of Canada, Foreign Investment Review Agency, A comparison of foreign investment controls in Canada and Australia, FRIA Papers No. 5. (Ottawa: April 1979), pp. 6-7.

38. See Chapter 9.

39. "Economic Briefs," World Business Weekly 2 (May 21, 1979): p. 54.

40. "The Business Society: Discrimination of foreign-owned companies leads to less employment," News from the Federation of Swedish Industries, no. 2 (May 1979): p. 1.

41. Ibid. , p. 2.

42. Ibid. , p. 2.

43. A. T. Kearney International, Ltd. , United States Manufacturing Investment in Japan: Executive Summary (Tokyo: The American Chamber of Commerce in Japan, July 1979), p. 3.

44. Robert Gilpin, United States Power and the Multinational Corporation: The Political Economy of Foreign Direct Investment (New York: Basic Books, 1975), pp. 111, 145.

45. Raymond Vernon and Louis T. Wells, Jr. , Manager in the International Economy, 3rd ed. (Englewood Cliffs: Prentice Hall, 1976), p. 89.

46. Sueo Sikiguchi, Japanese Direct Foreign Investment, Atlantic Institute for International Affairs Research Volume (London: MacMillan Press, 1979), p. 13.

47. "Japanese Bill to Alter Laws for Investment and Foreign Exchange," Wall Street Journal, December 12, 1979, p. 14.

48. Japan, Ministry of Finance, Outline of Amendments to both the Foreign Exchange and Foreign Trade Control Law (May 1979), p. 4.

49. Japan, Ministry of Finance, Essence of the bill to revise the Foreign Exchange and Foreign Trade Control Law (May 1979), pp. 5-7.

50. "Asia/Pacifica," Business International 26 (April 27, 1979): p. 136.

51. Sekiguchi, Japanese Investment, p. 136.

52. U. S. , General Accounting Office, Perspectives on Trade and International Payments, ID79-11A (October 10, 1979), p. 40.

53. James C. Abbegglen, "The Japan-U. S. Trade Crisis," The Wheel Extended, Special Supplement No. 4 (Spring 1979): p. 8.

54. Great Britain, Department of Trade and Industry, The Im-

pact of Foreign Direct Investment in the United Kingdom, M. D. Steuer et al., SBN 115110550 (London: Her Majesty's Stationery Office, 1973), pp. 10, 104.

55. Paul Streeten, "Multinationals revisited," Finance and Development 16 (June 1979): p. 40; and Katz, "International Investment," p. 181.

56. Garth Stevenson, The Control of Foreign Direct Investment in a Federation: Canadian and Australian Experience, Transnational Corporations Research Project, Research Monograph no. 3 (Sydney, Australia: University of Sydney, July 1976), p. 21.

57. A. E. Safarian and Joel Bell, "Issues Raised by Multinational Enterprise," in Multinational Corporations and Government: Business Government Relations in an International Context, eds. Patrick M. Boarman and Hans Schollhammer (New York: Praeger, 1975), p. 83.

58. Jeremy Howell, "A cry from the heart of England," Business Location File 3, no. 4 (1979): p. 19; for responses, see British Location File 3, no. 5 (1979): pp. 4-6.

59. Sam Allis, "Regions: States Pay Dearly, Gain Little in Competition to Lure Industry," Wall Street Journal, July 1, 1980, p. 25.

60. "Should we lure foreign investors?" World Business Weekly 2 (June 25, 1979): p. 7.

61. Ibid., p. 8.

62. Cohen, Foreign Direct Investment, pp. 9-2, 9-3.

63. ". . . it is worth noting that a major attraction for foreign companies is the current relative freedom of action in the United States. Our lack of advance approvals, of registration, of separate treatment of foreign as distinct from native companies is virtually unique in the world. Altering that picture for any but the most compelling reasons of national security or other vital national interest, in our personal views, would be unfortunate." Letter from David Bauer and James Greene, Conference Board to Hon. Benjamin Rosenthal, Chairman, Commerce, Consumer and Monetary Affairs Subcommittee, Committee on Government Operations, House, November 16, 1979 in U.S., Congress, House, Subcommittee of Committee on Government Operations, The Operations of Federal Agencies in Monitoring, Reporting on, and Analyzing Foreign Investments in the United States: Hearings, Part 3, 96th Cong., 1st sess., 1979, p. 563.

6

DIRECT CONTROLS: AN OVERVIEW

ECONOMIC BENEFITS

Although there are potential economic benefits from locational controls, there has been negligible legislative action or consideration in the United States. However, controls need not totally replicate the Western European programs, but could be tailored to the indigenous American business environment and could have specialized or limited applicability.

The direct controls that are operational in Western Europe have a high degree of flexibility because the criteria for approval are not precisely delineated. During prosperous periods when expansion and growth takes place, the controls to direct industry to impacted areas are very effective. On the other hand, in recession periods when there is strong subnational opposition to any potential loss of employment, the criteria can be eased.

It is easier to relax controls than to abandon them, and then have to use the legislative process to reinstate them. Officials in impacted areas are loathe to see controls dropped and would resist this kind of move. Politically, once abandoned, they are difficult to revive.

The costs of administering control systems are extremely low, particularly when compared with the costs of financial incentives. Even though this volume has stressed controls, it is important to realize that financial incentives have to work in unison with the controls.

A prerequisite to effective administration is the availability and recruiting of skilled personnel who can evaluate each case on its merits from a business as well as a regional and national viewpoint. Given the present level of government salaries, and the criticisms of public employees, it would not be easy to recruit such individuals in the United States.

ACCEPTANCE OF SITES IN INNER CITIES

The most questionable aspect of direct locational controls is private sector acceptance of sites in problem-ridden cities. In Britain prior to 1977 when the policy was reversed, the emphasis was on channeling industry out of prosperous regions with little concern for their inner cities; even within problem regions, inner cities can be overlooked. Controls coordinated with regional boundaries do not necessarily direct industry into inner cities. Given the choice of locating anywhere within a fairly large area, management can comply with the controls without placing facilities in inner cities. In the United Kingdom, there have been demands that regional preference be re-placed by preference for inner cities.[1] The "broadbrush" approach to designating areas is considered unfair by the English cities' advocate, the Association of Metropolitan Authorities. The organization wants to change both the United Kingdom and the European Economic Community regional policies so that the large cities in England would receive greater assistance.[2]

The conditions endemic to inner cities are unique and of such magnitude that they have been highly resistant to many diverse solutions including regionally-based programs. Attempts to guide or persuade industry even with generous financial subsidies are not likely to be effective in reversing the disinvestment process and, especially, the decline of manufacturing. The growth in office and service jobs is occurring outside the inner city. Management is understandably reluc-tant to place facilities in inner cities because of the adverse social and environmental conditions.

It is not necessary that firms locate within inner cities for the residents to benefit. Locational controls need not limit firms to inner cities in order to offer job opportunities; a location accessible to the inner city could be a compromise that forestalls or mitigates the strong business opposition to establishing operations within inner cities. The assumption that inner city problems will be solved largely within inner cities in questionable; ". . . current inner city problems will not be solved within the boundaries of the inner city but only in the context of planning activities elsewhere within the city region."[3] Not all deprived individuals reside in inner cities and there may be a degree of inequity in only considering their job needs instead of giving equal consideration to those of the deprived within a larger area.[4] The solution is more likely to emanate from a broad geographic con-text which encompasses inner cities.

> . . . within a broader regional context it can be argued
> that any industrial, employment growth is going to
> benefit the region regardless of where it is. To there-
> fore promote growth in the most attractive locations . . .
> is the obvious first step. Similarly, the inner city prob-
> lem has to be seen on a much broader scale—any poli-
> cies promoted by the local authority are only tinkering
> with the symptoms—the underlying causes are linked to
> much broader political and economic considerations
> which need to be tackled nationally.[5]

POTENTIAL OBSTACLES

The relevance of controls decline when areas that are too small
or too large are designated as development or assisted areas. The
British Government's plans to create enterprise zones has received
much attention in the United States, and has led to the introduction of
the Urban Jobs and Enterprise Zone Act in Congress. It would give
liberal benefits to business locating in enterprise zones within urban
centers.

> The bill . . . raises a . . . profound set of questions
> about whether development efforts for distressed areas
> should target subjurisdictions and neighborhoods, as
> this bill does. It is not at all certain that the most
> effective method of improving a neighborhood is to
> create a favorable environment for business growth
> only within that neighborhood. Nor is it clear that
> community governments, which have their own con-
> cept of where local development should take place,
> will find their planning goals consistent with the loca-
> tional requirements of the Enterprise Zone legislation.
> Thus, the attempt to define a precise zone may fail
> to respond to the needs of an area.[6]

The larger the area, the more likely it is that there will be
pockets which do not correspond to the area's overall depressed condition. Boundaries must be kept flexible but not to the extent that it
is extremely risky for corporate management to plan for investment
on a particular site. Management has to have reasonable assurance
that, by complying with government rules, its proposals will be
acceptable to the authorities. "No industrialist can afford to risk
premature expenditure if there is a chance of the project being
rejected."[7]

Because transnational corporations can operate from many countries, the controls applied to these firms are limited. The United States has great, though not total, freedom in restricting these firms by virtue of the large internal market and geographic separation.

A deterrent to instituting programs to guide industry in the United States is the primary loyalty of Congress to their constituencies in preference to a national viewpoint. In Western Europe members of parliaments have a more national perspective and are more responsive to party wishes than to local pressures. However, controls or directives do not have to be imposed only through legislation; as indicated by the Community Conservation Guidelines, executive or presidential action may be applied in a limited sense.

There could be greater acceptance if controls were applied to new foreign investment. Ironically, though foreign firms may have wide flexibility in terms of national boundaries, they have less concern about placing new facilities in depressed areas. They have no roots or ties to a particular locality or area, and no problems with relocating or dismissing employees, or with divesting existing plants and equipment.

INDUSTRY FOR IMPACTED AREAS

Industrial development policies and programs have concentrated on the secondary (manufacturing) sector. But the tertiary (service) and quaternary (high technology, research and development) sectors are now the growth sectors. However, the ability of many impacted areas to attract these kinds of industries is limited. Though the tertiary and quaternary activities would make the greatest contribution to industrial development, these areas often lack the necessary degree of geographic centrality, adequate infrastructure, amenities and the skilled labor force demanded by corporate management.

In a depressed regional economy, from a short-range standpoint, there is neither the freedom nor the luxury to await the arrival of service and high-technology industries that would provide diversification and avoid overdependence on one industry or on declining industries.

> . . . though there is undoubtedly some (and small) scope
> for applying regional policy to the service sector, measures in this field are unlikely to provide a substitute
> for policies in the industrial field. [8]

Over a longer period of time, there should be planning to break the excessive reliance on low-growth or technologically backward industries as a means of gradually attaining the proper industrial mixture. One source of revitalization is the channeling of government contracts, particularly defense, to depressed areas; however, there has been limited success in realizing this goal.

Delays in remedial action further undermine the desirability to corporate management of sites in depressed regions. A continuing exodus of industry leads to a deterioration in the skills of the labor force[9] and a decline in the condition of the social and physical infrastructure.

Locational controls have the potential to prevent or forestall the cumulative and devastating effects of continuing decline. Consideration should be given not only to legislative acceptability, but also to cost effectiveness and the ability of industry to operate efficiently only in a limited number of areas. Controls have largely been governed by political and employment factors, which are generally separated from the optimum and economic uses of resources and land.[10] Industrial policy could be a means of reconciliation.

All indications point to the development or formulation of a national industrial policy to revitalize the lagging United States economy. To attain any appreciable progress, industry will have to be in optimum locations in terms of costs and productivity. A massive federal role is anticipated in rebuilding industry and infrastructure. In a variation or adaptation of existing direct controls, the government will have a lever to rebuild depressed regional economies while simultaneously reconstructing the national economy.

NOTES

1. Allen R. Townsend, "The Relationship of Inner City Problems to Regional Policy," Regional Studies 11, no. 4 (1977): p. 226.

2. "Big Cities Call for More Community Cash," Inside Europe, National Council for Voluntary Organizations (June 1980): p. 3.

3. Martin Horne, "A Reappraisal of the New Towns," in Town and Country Planning Summer School, University of Saint Andrews, Report of Proceedings (Royal Town Planning Institute: London, September 1-13, 1978), p. 23.

4. Ray Pahl, "Will the Inner City Problem Ever Go Away?," in Town and Country Planning Summer School, University of Saint Andrews, Report of Proceedings (Royal Town Planning Institute: London, September 1-13, 1978), p. 9.

5. Regional Studies Association, West Midlands Branch, Working Party on Inner City Programmes and Regional Strategies, untitled paper (May 1978), p. 11.

6. Northeast-Midwest Institute, Tax Cuts for Business: Will They Help Distressed Areas? (Washington, D.C.: September 1980), prepared by Mary Fitzpatrick and Peter Trooper, p. 50.

7. Slough Estates Ltd., Industrial Investment—A Case Study in Factory Building (Slough: April 1979), p. 11.

8. Organization for Economic Cooperation and Development, Regional Policies and the Services Sector (Paris: 1978), p. 42.

9. After the plant shutdowns in Youngstown, Ohio, employers from the South and West advertised for skilled workers. Tool and die makers who require from eight to nine years on-the-job training were leaving; this compounded the difficulties of attracting replacement industry. Marguerite Beck-Rex, "Youngstown, Can This Steel City Forge a Comeback," Planning (United States) 44 (January 1978): p. 13.

10. Slough Estates Ltd., Industrial Investment, p. 11.

PART II

INDIRECT CONTROLS

7

CODETERMINATION: THE EFFECT
ON LOCATIONAL DECISIONS

MODELS OF CODETERMINATION

A Basis for Assessment

Though codetermination has received extensive attention in this country, a key aspect has been largely overlooked in the United States; codetermination can have a long-range impact on the location of industry, i.e. the closing or moving of facilities and employees. A basis for an assessment is emerging in Western Europe, particularly in the Federal Republic of Germany. West Germany has been the pacesetter and is serving as a model for other countries and regions, such as the European Economic Community which is considering the enactment of codetermination legislation.

Codetermination, in terms of this examination, is concerned primarily with employee representation on supervisory boards which are the equivalent of boards of directors in U.S. corporations. The supervisory boards' authority and decision making are subordinate only to that of shareholders. Because of the differences over codetermination, a commission appointed by the West German government to make long-range recommendations felt that a precise definition was necessary to start their work:

The institutional participation of the employees or their representatives in the formation and contents of the process of will and decision making in the enterprise, here

without regard to the type and extent of participation
by employees' representatives in the organs of the
enterprise [collective bargaining].[1]

Collective Bargaining and Codetermination

A fundamental difference between collective bargaining and codetermination, though the objectives and results may be similar, is
that under codetermination employee representatives are involved and
informed in the decision-making process.[2] Under collective bargaining,
labor is usually involved at a later stage after a decision has already
been made; their reaction may be limited to efforts to overturn or
delay implementation. Collective bargaining does not encompass the
range of decisions considered under codetermination.

> [collective bargaining]. . . leaves a wide range of
> fundamental managerial decisions affecting work-
> people that are beyond the control . . . and very
> largely beyond the influence—of workpeople and their
> trade unions. Major decisions on investment, loca-
> tion, closures, takeovers and mergers, and product
> specialization of the organization are generally
> taken at levels where collective bargaining does not
> take place, and indeed are subject matter not readily
> covered by collective bargaining . . . There therefore
> needs to be an examination of how workers' organi-
> zations could exert a degree of control over planning
> and policymaking.[3]

PROGRESS IN THE UNITED STATES

Labor Interest

Labor unions in the United States have shown little interest in
the adoption of codetermination, as illustrated by the widely quoted
May 1976 statement of Thomas R. Donahue, Secretary-Treasurer,
who was then executive assistant to the President of the AFL-CIO,

> We do not seek to be a partner in management—to be,
> most likely, the junior partner in success and the senior
> partner in failure.

We do not want to blur in any way the distinctions between the respective roles of management and labor in the plant.

We regard our independence fiercely—independent of government, independent of any political party and independent of management.

We've watched codetermination and its offshoot experiments with interest, and will continue to do so, but it is our judgment that it offers little to American unions in the performance of their job unionism role (given our exclusive representative status and our wide-open conflict bargaining) and it could only hurt U.S. unions as they pursue their social unionism functions— seeing through legislation, political action, community involvement and a host of other approaches, to improve our members' lot by improving society generally.[4]

Demands for Representation

Until 1979, proposals to have union representation on company boards of directors had made little progress. At one time the corporation laws of several states permitted the election of directors by employees; they could vote separately from the shareholders if permitted by the corporate charter or bylaws. Both the Massachusetts General Laws chapter 156 (1932) and the New Jersey Revised Statutes 14.9-1 to -3 (1957), which allowed such elections, have been repealed.[5] Phillip Murray, who was then vice-president of the CIO, and Morris Cooke, a consulting engineer and proponent of scientific management, suggested in their 1940 book that one or more union officials be seated on company boards of directors, but their advice was largely ignored.[6] At the 1972 annual meeting of United Air Lines the pilots sought board representation, their objective was to improve channels of communication rather than to participate in decision making. They received only 5 percent of the vote and had no support from the Airline Pilots Association. In 1973, the Providence and Worcester Railroad agreed to have labor representation on the board of directors for its 20 workers. In the same year, the United Rubber Workers wanted the General Tire and Rubber Company to appoint a union member to its board, but the company opposed the move.[7] During the 1976 contract negotiations, the teamsters reportedly demanded without success the seating of two union representatives on the board of Anheuser Busch.[8] Inspired by the offer of Chrysler's UK subsidiary to allow worker directors, the United Automobile Workers

(UAW) in 1976 requested two seats on the company's board. The union sought to achieve this through collective bargaining but dropped the demand because of Chrysler's opposition.

A Breakthrough for Worker Representation

A breakthrough with implications for corporate decisions on location occurred in 1979. In July the UAW as part of its bargaining demands called for worker representation on Chrysler's board of directors and for the establishment of committees of worker representatives at various levels. They "will have equal authority with management in reaching decisions of all types, including—but not limited to—those involving plant location/dislocation, product planning, capital spending, pricing policies, production planning, quality control, health and safety and overtime utilization."[9]

Later in the year, in the wake of Chrysler's financial crisis the company agreed to nominate Douglas Fraser, UAW president, to the board of directors. If elected, he had no intentions of representing the shareholders; instead he would speak for the union and the public. Initially, other UAW officers were cool to union representation on the corporate board, but the surprising decision to close the Hamtramck, Michigan assembly plant, which employed 5,000 members, changed their minds. Mr. Fraser conceded he could not have reversed the decision, but he might have had the plant phased out over a longer period, or he would have done more to see that workers found new jobs. "Maybe that way you can moderate a decision." It is difficult to envision abstaining from voting on issues that affect workers since there are not likely to be too many unrelated issues. On issues that affect his members he intends to be the workers' advocate but not vote. When asked about his strategy on collective bargaining he replied, "I'll just walk out of the room." Maintaining its traditional bargaining practices, the UAW may eventually move to seek representation on the General Motors and Ford boards. The GM chairman, Thomas A. Murphy, strongly criticized the Chrysler move and stated there would be strong company opposition to the appointment of worker directors.[10]

The 1980 settlement between the American Motors Corporation (AMC) and the UAW called for a conditional agreement on one board seat for a UAW member. The legality of appointing a labor representative was subject to the approval of the Federal Trade Commission and the Departments of Justice and Labor. There was also concern about the potential conflict of interest from the UAW president's membership on the board of Chrysler, which is an AMC competitor.[11]

MULTINATIONAL CORPORATIONS AND UNIONS

In the United States and many other countries, business and labor are being placed in the position whereby codetermination can no longer be ignored. As will be seen in the Volkswagen plan to establish facilities in the United States, codetermination in one country has ramifications even in those countries without codetermination. About 40 of the 600 to 650 companies subject to codetermination in Germany are U.S. companies, such as Ford, General Motors, IBM, Proctor and Gamble, and Sperry Rand.

According to the chairman and chief executive officer, J. Paul Lyett, Sperry Rand has learned to work with codetermination in West Germany and, in fact, has turned it to the company's advantage. The new board members, who are very intelligent, understand the problems facing the company and have been instrumental in communicating them to employees. The disadvantage for companies resulting from worker directors has been the disproportionately high rise in supplementary benefits added to regular wages and salaries. Lyett concludes that codetermination is a very real possibility for the United States; perhaps it will evolve more slowly as compared to Europe because fewer U.S. workers belong to unions and a labor political party is lacking.

> It may take on different forms than it does in Europe, but the persistence of unemployment and inflation here is bound to produce more interest in codetermination. Labor leaders will be working hard with their constituents, with Congress and with regulatory agencies to give momentum to some form of worker participation.[12]

On the management side, foreign subsidiaries and joint ventures bring the firm closer to involvement in codetermination. On the labor side, multinational unionism is growing. For example, the West German subsidiaries of DuPont, ITT, Philips, and Ford face the prospect of having international trade unionists, including non-Germans, on their supervisory boards. In effect, this is a demand by European trade unions for a transnational voice; representatives of employees of multinational enterprises want to be involved in global investment, including disinvestment, principally because of the employment implications. In contrast, North American unions responded in a survey that they were not pleased with sharing responsibility with management on investment decisions. "In this particular context, they saw difficulties in reconciling European ideas of 'participation' with the North American approach to collective bargaining with an employer."[13]

TABLE 7.1

West German Codetermination Legislation—Chronology

Date	Title	Description
1891	Work protection legis-lation (Arbeitsschutz-gesetz)	Provided for the creation of worker committees with participation rights in the development of shop procedures and welfare provisions (Mitwirkungs-recht)
1905 & 1909	Revisions of Prussian mining legislation (Novellen zum Pr. Berggesetz)	Extended committee par-ticipation in safety regu-lation extended to de facto codetermination
1916, 1917	Defense industry legis-lation (Vaterlandischer Hilfsdienst)	Further extension of par-ticipatory rights of worker committees; joint produc-tion committees
1919	Article 165, Weimar Constitution	Provides for the develop-ment of a system of works and regional worker coun-cils, national economy council
1920	Works council law (Betriebsrategesetz)	Works council is given codetermination rights for work procedures and re-dundancy policies in fac-tories with at least 20 employees
1922	Extension of Corpora-tion Law (Novelle sum Aktien-Gesellschafts-recht)	At least one seat on supervisory board re-served for works-council member
1951	Montan Codetermina-tion Law (Montan Mit-bestimmungsgesetz)	Gives employees 50 per-cent of supervisory board seats. Three-fifths na-tional union functionaries, only two-fifths actual em-ployees. Valid only in coal-iron-steel industry

(continued)

TABLE 7.1 (continued)

Date	Title	Description
1952	Works Council of 1952 (1952 Betriebsverfass-ungsgesetz)	Consists of two parts: (1) Works legislation (2) Enterprise legislation. (1) Established works council; codetermination rights in establishing work, promotion, and layoff rules; (2) Gives employees one-third of supervisory board seats. No outside representatives permitted; no specific role for union
1972	Works Council Law of 1972 (1972 Betriebs-verfassungsgesetz)	Extends the codetermination rights of the works council. Defines relationship between local unions and works councils; strengthens position of unions vis-à-vis works councils
1976	(Reform) Codetermination Law of 1976 (Mitbestimmungsge-setz, 1976)	Reforms the "enterprise" legislation of the 1952 law. Employees receive 50 percent of the supervisory board seats, but the chairman, chosen by stockholders, has two votes in case of tie. Role of union strengthened. Depending on size of supervisory board, 1/3, 1/4, or 3/10ths of employee seats reserved for "outside," national union functionaries. Applies only to firms with over 2,000 employees. For firms with less than 2,000 employees, the 1952 legislation remains intact.

Source: Alfred L. Thimm, The Origins of Codetermination: 1848-1949, Administrative and Engineering Systems Monograph AES 7806 (Schenectady: Union College and University, December 1977), pp. 36-37.

Many trade union leaders in Europe feel that decisions by headquarters concerning investment and production rationalization have greater consequences for workers than the traditional issues of wages, fringe benefits and working conditions.

> The really substantive decisions, they say are made in the very remote and inaccessible headquarters of the multinational firm and they want worker representatives to have a say in those decisions, as well, as in those which are generally left to subsidiary managers. [14]

To limit the power of multinationals, the main EEC labor organization, the European Trade Union Confederation, drafted an EEC-wide law that would obligate worker participation in management at the parent company level.[15] The EEC Labor Affairs Commissioner has been seeking regulations, exclusive of codetermination, that would mandate companies to notify employees of all significant decisions on corporate strategy prior to their effectuation.[16]

WEST GERMAN CODETERMINATION LEGISLATION

The legislative origins of West German codetermination go back to 1891. (See Table 7.1). There are three major pieces of legislation in effect mandating codetermination beginning with the Codetermination Act of 1951. This legislation covers the montan (coal, iron and steel) industry; the supervisory board consists of 11, 15 or 21 members. For example, on a board with eleven members, there are five shareholder representatives, five labor representatives, and the eleventh person is chosen jointly by the other ten members. The labor side consists of two company employees (one blue-collar and one white-collar) and three nominated by the unions not necessarily employees of the company. In practice national union leaders have selected the employee representatives.

In 1952, legislation was enacted extending codetermination to firms outside montan but giving employees only one-third of the seats on supervisory boards for companies with 500 to 2,000 employees. The labor representatives have tended to be employees rather than outside union officials.

The 1976 Codetermination Act, which went into effect in July 1978, applies to firms with over 2,000 employees. According to the size of the firm, the supervisory board consists of 12, 16 or 20 members; half are employee representatives and the other half are stockholder representatives. Labor representatives consist of employees and outside trade unionists in the proportion of 4 to 2, 6 to 2 or 7 to 3, depending on the total number of employees.

One of the employee members is elected by the managerial employees. The chairman is elected by a two-thirds majority vote. If the two-thirds is not attained, the shareholder representatives make the selection. Subsequently, when there is a tie vote, the chairman has two votes to break the deadlock. Union officials contend these provisions make parity on supervisory boards impossible.

The supervisory board does not manage but does select the members of the management board which runs the company. There are three mandated corporate groups: the general stockholder or shareholder meeting; the supervisory board which is the equivalent of the U.S. board of directors; and the management board which is the equivalent of the U.S. top management.

THE WEST GERMAN HARD COAL INDUSTRY

Influence of Codetermination

The most spectacular series of closings and reorganizations that have occurred under codetermination to date have been in the West German hard coal industry between 1958 and 1968. The scope of the cutback is indicated by the reduction in the number of miners from 578,000 in 1951 to 300,000 in 1969, approximately 50 percent.[17] As an example for other industries affected by codetermination, the coal industry obviously differs because of its inability to relocate facilities.

There are conflicting viewpoints on the influence of codetermination in generating and resolving the coal crisis. Proponents of codetermination assert that it proved extremely valuable in the smoothness and peacefulness of the transition; while opponents claim that it was partially responsible for the crisis by preventing early action and resolution of the problems facing the industry.

Union officials claim restructuring of the hard coal industry went so smoothly because of codetermination and the influence of unions on the worker representatives. This assertion has been supported by a close observer of codetermination in West Germany, Alfred L. Thimm, Director of the Institute of Administration and Management, and Professor of Economics and Industrial Administration at Union College:

On the supervisory boards the union leaders cooperated with management to obtain employee and stockholder representatives' cooperation in closing inefficient mines and factories, and in channeling all investment into the most efficient location. Quite clearly, the employee representatives were reluctant to vote for the closing of "their" factories while the union leaders could and did keep regional and national interests in mind. There is little doubt that the responsibility and good sense displayed by the German coal and steel union leadership during the 1950's made a major contribution to Germany's economic recovery and, in the long run, to the economic well being of the union members. [18]

A Favorable View of Codetermination

A favorable view of codetermination in the coal industry was expressed in the 1970 report by the prestigious Biedenkopf Commission as part of its recommendations leading to the enactment of the 1976 codetermination law. The government-appointed commission consisted of nine professors, chaired by Kurt Biedenkopf, who was then rector of the University of Bochum. He subsequently became secretary of the Christian Democratic Union, a basically conservative political party. The Commission questioned 55 persons, including spokesmen for capital and labor in coal and steel and other industries. Questionnaires were sent to 62 coal and steel companies and to 373 other companies affected by codetermination; there was an 86 percent response.[19] The Commission noted that codetermination in the montan industry resulted in some postponement in arriving at decisions to cut capacity and close facilities, but it did not lead to an outright rejection of the suggestions and objectives of enterprise management.[20]

The Commission observed that heavy government aid to the coal industry and to laid-off workers eased any strains on the system. The assistance to industry was in the form of import duties, quotas and freight subsidies. The cost to the government for the mine closings in 1968 at prevailing exchange rates was the equivalent of $268 million. The Commission commented that codetermination does not prevent streamlining of considerable magnitude and need not adversely affect productivity. The index of coal production per hour worked rose from 100 in 1962 to 143 in 1968, outperforming the national industrial average of 142.7. The index of iron production also increased above the national average to 145.5.[21]

A factor in the successful management-labor cooperation was the informal caucuses in which information was exchanged and alternatives were evaluated. Only when a consensus had been reached was it submitted to the supervisory board for final approval. Controversial topics seldom come to the board unless a compromise had already been agreed upon. The early difficulties at Volkswagen have been attributed to the lack of such a procedure.[22]

The 50 percent decline in employment in the coal industry did not result in any appreciable social unrest and financial burden on the workers who accepted what was economically necessary. The companies with government cooperation were able to allow workers ample time and opportunity to readjust while receiving adequate compensation. Without the government assistance, undoubtedly the cutbacks would not have been so readily accepted by the workers.

FOREIGN INVESTMENT IN WEST GERMANY

Another viewpoint is that codetermination in the montan industry indicates potential weakness in the West German economy:

> If its critics are right and codetermination is responsible
> for depriving the coal, iron and steel industries of the
> flexibility to close down unprofitable product lines, plants,
> unproductive facilities and venture into new lines in other
> communities, then codetermination when applied to vir-
> tually all of Germany's major industrial plants may mark
> the end of the German "economic miracle." Indeed some
> informed observers believe that codetermination has
> already been a factor in channelizing German investment
> capital into other countries.[23]

The critics have not been entirely correct in their assessment.[24] The West German "economic miracle" did not end; the fears about Germany's desirability as an investment site did not come to pass. A survey of 39 German multinationals and the 34 largest subsidiaries of foreign companies was prepared for the West German Economic Ministry; it indicated that foreign companies, particularly U.S. companies, feel the only negative investment factor is the 1976 Co-determination Act.[25] Codetermination is not the only determinant of the investment decision but is one item in an imprecise cost-benefit evaluation.

> To what extent, if at all, national codetermination laws
> can motivate foreign companies to relocate or to limit
> future investment depends on a number of factors. De-
> spite restricted corporate freedom of decision, the rele-
> vant country may still offer cost and other advantages,

unless equally profitable access to its markets exists
indirectly from other locations not governed by codetermination laws. In general, codetermination regulations should not initiate an exodus of foreign corporation
production facilities, but they could motivate foreign
companies to look for equivalent alternatives without
codetermination for future investment, especially if
they exist within a common market. [26]

WEST GERMAN INVESTMENT ABROAD

Volkswagen in the United States

Investment abroad from a West German perspective is likely to
become more controversial and encounter growing resistance on the
part of workers under codetermination who, to preserve their jobs,
will seek to direct investment to domestic facilities. [27] Yet, an American labor specialist finds it "eminently reasonable that corporations
seeking to establish production facilities abroad should be required to
discuss their plans with the organizations representing their employees
prior to taking final decisions . . . and would like to see the employee
representatives armed with the same power they have under German
codetermination. The unions might object to any and all investments
that meant loss of jobs, but they would be on much weaker ground where
the investment was essential to maintain the firm's viability, as it
might be where semiskilled labor intensive production was involved." [28]

A prime example of the impact of codetermination on investment
abroad is the Volkswagen decision to establish facilities in the United
States despite the opposition from certain groups on the supervisory
board. "As a result German and foreign managers will now be prompted
to analyze past experience with employee participation and also to
reassess management behavior in state-owned or state-controlled
enterprises." [29]

Volkswagen was established in 1937 by the National Socialist
government and was resurrected in 1948 as a state enterprise and
remained this way until 1972. The Conservative-Liberal government
wanted to sell shares to the private sector, but opposition to this
proposal caused 60 percent of the shares to be sold to the public, while
20 percent was allotted to the state of Lower Saxony, and 20 percent
was retained by the federal government.

All West German governments since 1937 have used Volkswagen facilities as a means of industrializing the backward areas of
the country. As part of this policy, the main plant of the company was

situated in 1937 in Wolfsburg, a small town of only 1,000 people in a poor agricultural area in the northern part of West Germany. By 1979 the population reached 130,000. Subsequently, other problem areas were selected for plant sites along the East German border and in East Frisia. The price of a hands-off policy by the state and federal governments from 1948 to 1968 was management's cooperation with the government's long-range regional policy.

Long-range Outlook for Volkswagen

Until the 1970s, the Volkswagen success story hid the contradictions between the demands of a long-range regional development policy and the market impositions on a profit-based enterprise. The location of Volkswagen facilities in marginal areas affected not only production costs but also made the recently industrialized areas overly dependent on the company's fortunes. Therefore, workers were likely to resist any shift of facilities or expansion elsewhere, especially overseas. But the heavy reliance on exports raised questions about the outlook for domestic production.

In 1968, almost 70 percent of output was exported, with about 40 percent going to the United States; the head of the U.S. subsidiary felt that to maintain its market position, Volkswagen should have a production or assembly line in the United States. Leiding, the Volkswagen chief at that time, recognized and agreed with this assessment and began to think of either starting production in the United States or entering into a cooperative agreement with a U.S. manufacturer; however, Leiding, a determined production man, never was aware of or took into consideration the growing importance of the workers' power.[30] In May 1974, he announced approval of the establishment of a manufacturing facility in the United States as a means of reducing freight costs and overcoming exchange difficulties. He first obtained the support of his management team and informed only certain supervisory board members of his plans; this secrecy compounded his problems.

In 1952, the codetermination law mandated companies to submit any major relocation plans to the supervisory board which then consisted of 21 members. One-third were employee directors dominated by the trade union representative, Eugen Loderer, head of the powerful metal workers union, I.G. Metall, and vice-chairman of the board, who played a major role in arriving at a compromise. The union was particularly concerned with maintaining Volkswagen's position as a pacesetter for wages and working conditions.

Two of the fourteen capital representatives came from the federal government in Bonn, and two came from the State of Lower Saxony; despite their 40 percent ownership of Volkswagen, they were not totally concerned with profit maximization. A fifth capital member was the chairman of the management board of a union-owned bank. Thus, labor had a possible voting majority.

The loss by the company of over $500 million in 1973 and 1974 and the inability to obtain union assent for production in the United States forced Leiding to resign. [31] There was strong resistance by the union and the State of Lower Saxony because of the potential loss of jobs. The dominant economic sector in the State remains auto manufacturing, notably Volkswagen in Wolfsburg, which employs almost 20 percent of the labor force; in addition numerous firms are suppliers to the industry. [32]

Approval of United States Plant

On April 1976, the supervisory board unanimously approved the investment of $250 million in a U.S. plant. The concurrence of I.G. Metall and the worker directors was forthcoming only after certain conditions were agreed upon: supervisory board approval would be necessary for any increases in the amount of U.S. components in any cars assembled in the U.S. from the original 65 percent or for any change in employment resulting from the U.S. project; no cars assembled in the United States would be exported to Germany; DM 40 million (about $16 million) was pledged by Volkswagen to retool the Emden plant which was producing Rabbit models for export to the U.S.; this would enable operations to be continued in the plant after the loss of the U.S. market; and labor was given guarantees that employment levels would be maintained for ten years.

After the agreement was reached on the U.S. project, incorporation of the Volkswagen subsidiary in the U.S. was established in a way that the supervisory board in West Germany oversees operations of the U.S. company, and any expansion of the U.S. operation must be approved by the supervisory board. This method gives the trade union important leverage to bargain with corporations about relocation and new site plans. In contrast to the protracted negotiations for the first plant in the United States, the Volkswagen supervisory board in April 1980 endorsed plans for the second United States plant without conflict.

BOARD REPRESENTATION IN TRANSNATIONAL OPERATIONS

With the new Volkswagen plant in Pennsylvania operational and the UAW successful in organizing the employees, the complexities and

relationships of transnational operations and codetermination should
emerge. What position will the U.S. employees and trade unions have
in the parent company's supervisory board? How will the UAW and
I. G. Metall interact? The first UAW contract negotiated in 1978 at
Volkswagen's New Stanton, Pennsylvania assembly plant gave no
indication nor contained any mention of codetermination. [33]

The potential impact of codetermination in the United States is
illustrated by various transnational arrangements that are being
planned. One of these arrangements is the trend toward a world car
with major parts produced in locations throughout the world, assem-
bled at several points, and sold throughout the world with only minor
style changes, e.g., Ford's Fiesta and GM's Chevette. "The inter-
nationalization of the world's auto industry is beginning to be viewed
as inevitable." [34]

What started as a joint distribution and production plan between
Renault, the French state-owned auto maker, and AMC ended with
Renault taking effective control of AMC. [35] In 1979, Renault established financial and production links with Mack Trucks. As a wholly
state-owned company, Renault is mandated to have a tripartite supervisory board with one-third of the members each from trade unions,
management, and government, and all have equal voting rights.

Other West European auto companies—MAN and Mercedes Benz
of West Germany, Volvo of Sweden, and IVECO of Italy and West
Germany have negotiated for the production, assembly, or distribution
of trucks in the United States. As these transactions are consummated,
companies will have to face the same question that Volkswagen did. Will
some form of board representation for the workers and trade unions in
the United States follow transnational arrangements?

WORKER DIRECTORS AND INVESTMENT

Characteristics of Worker Directors

Since 1951, when the codetermination legislation was effectuated,
certain features have emerged. The employee representatives drawn
from the work force have been much more parochial in their viewpoint
than have been the union officials serving on supervisory boards. The
officials have demonstrated a greater awareness and understanding of
management's needs and have been more prone to work with management in resolving the broader economic and industrial problems facing
the company. The rank and file workers frequently lack the background
to cope with much of the supervisory board agenda and are placed in

a difficult position, often one of inferiority, in deciding on matters for which they are untrained.

The Biedenkopf Commission found the attitudes of employee representatives from the plants toward cutbacks, transfers in production and closings too narrowly focused. To compensate for this weakness in codetermination, the Commission recommended that employee representatives not be drawn exclusively from the work force. [36]

Pressures on Worker Directors

The worker directors as a group are generally active proponents of investment or expansion that purportedly strengthen the company and increase employment security. They are under great pressure to resist any actions that could adversely affect workers. In time worker representatives see the need for such change and concentrate on insuring adequate social compensation for workers. One German firm needed five years to close a plant that was losing money because workers on the supervisory board forced debate and compromise every step of the way. [37] However, such delays are not common.

A former economics professor, Ulf A. Trolle, who has reorganized more than 50 Swedish companies, found the position of worker directors to be untenable because of divided loyalties.

> At first they are torn between what is good for their colleagues and what is good for the company. Then they start learning the problems of running a business and they start thinking like we do in management. They begin concurring on hard decisions, such as closing down a plant. Once that happens they simply lose their jobs. Twice, I have seen companies lose their most intelligent board members, because the workers refused to reelect them. [38]

Approval of Investments

The Biedenkopf Commission could find no case where employee representatives have refused to agree to investment projects or made the argument that available funds should rather be used for employee benefits rather than distributing as profits.

> The participation of employee representatives in investment decisions may. . . be expected to lead to

undesirable strengthening of the undertaking's preparedness to invest. Obstacles to investment measures
may therefore be expected only if jobs are saved
through new installations and other jobs of at least
equal status are not provided in exchange. [39]

Several factors could be damaging to the revitalization of a failing national economy as a result of codetermination there could be
delays in introducing new technology or innovation, or industry might
get locked into uneconomic sites and be forced to continue uneconomic
operations. The Biedenkopf Commission recognized that the workforce
will obviously tend to resist or postpone the loss of jobs or movement
of industry. However, delayed response to market forces could be
damaging to the economy as a whole in terms of growth. Thus, it is
in the best national interests for industry to reach agreement with
workers as expeditiously as possible in order to permit change to
take place.

Since future economic development will compel structural
changes and, consequently, closures and large-scale con-
versations as well, particular importance must be attached
to the potential tensions which will be institutionalized by
employee representatives occupying a number of the supervisory board seats. This situation of tension can be formally
summarized from the economic point of view as the juxta-
position of short-term employee interests in maintaining
and extending existing jobs and the long-term interests
in securing commercial growth by rational conduct on the
part of undertakings. [40]

DOMESTIC OUTLOOK FOR CODETERMINATION

A Foothold in the United States

What is the likelihood of codetermination gaining a foothold in
the United States? Because most unions assign low priority to instituting codetermination, there would appear to be little chance of
adoption in the foreseeable future. A prediction by Herman Rebhan,
general secretary of the International Metalworkers' Federation and
vice-chairman of the supervisory board of Ford's West German 57,000
employee subsidiary, Ford-Werke, is that within five years it will be
a "prestige matter" for American unions to have one of their officers
on the company board. [41]

U. S. labor unions will have to become involved, though not by choice or for prestige, as codetermination becomes more widespread in other countries and particularly if adopted by the European Economic Community. They will have to deal increasingly with transnational firms who have facilities in countries subject to codetermination as well as countries without codetermination, such as the U. S. It is questionable if the workers in the countries with codetermination will continue to have a voice on enterprise supervisory boards without U. S. workers demanding equal input into decisions that affect them.

Mobility of Industry

The principal effect of codetermination could be to presage the end or curtailment of entrepreneurial ability to be mobile. Firms will have to be extremely cautious in selecting locations since they no longer could make unilateral decisions on phasing out facilities. One factor resulting in fewer divestments by European than by U. S. firms is ". . .the increasing information rights and/or decision-sharing power granted to employees and their representatives, to unions and even to governments who have to be properly notified of major decisions (such as divestment) being considered by management. [42]

Firms from countries with codetermination will need ample time to arrive at decisions on foregin investment as employee representatives have first to be convinced that the workers' interests are being protected. Moves will become more costly as affected employees demand generous compensation for their consent.

Codetermination, albeit in a modified form, may not be completely removed from realization in the United States. A key component of the highly debated industrial policy is industry-labor cooperation for which codetermination provides a working model.

NOTES

1. Commission on Codetermination, Kurt W. Biedenkopf, Chairman, Codetermination in the Enterprise, English translation by the Anglo-German Foundation for the Study of Industrial Society (Bocum and London: January 1970), p. 2.

2. "While collective bargaining is undoubtedly itself a form of codetermination, it is a form which is reactive and adversarial rather than participatory and cooperative. It may not always represent the most effective means of insuring that the employee viewpoint is taken into account in the formulation of basic corporate policies and . . . a

large number of decisions of vital interest to employees remain beyond its scope." J. Bautz Bonanno, "Employee Codetermination: Origins in Germany, Present Practice in Europe, and Applicability to the United States," Harvard Journal on Legislation 14 (June 1977): p. 988.

3. Trades Union Congress, Industrial Democracy, p. 34, quoted in Ibid., p. 968.

4. Quoted by Milton Derber, "Collective Bargaining: The American Approach to Industrial Democracy," The Annals 431 (May 1977): p. 92.

5. Phillip I. Blumberg, "Reflections on Proposals for Corporate Reform Through Changes in the Composition of the Board of Directors: 'Special Interest' or 'Public' Directors," Boston University Law Review 53 (1973): p. 553.

6. Philip Murray and Morris Cooke, Organized Labor and Production: Next Steps in Industrial Democracy (New York: Harper & Row, 1940).

7. Blumberg, "Corporate Reform," p. 566.

8. Richard M. Steuer, "Employee Representation on the Board: Industrial Democracy or Interlocking Directorate," Columbia Journal of Transnational Law 16 (1977): p. 255.

9. News from the UAW, UAW Public Relations and Publications Department, July 27, 1979.

10. Robert L. Simison, "UAW's Fraser to Speak Out for Labor, Public in Role as Director of Chrysler," Wall Street Journal, October 29, 1979, p. 6; and "GM Chief Hits Chrysler's Plan to Seat Fraser," Wall Street Journal, November 8, 1979, p. 4.

11. "AMC Walkout Ends as UAW Accepts Accord," Wall Street Journal, September 19, 1980, p. 10.

12. "You are shooting at moving targets when establishing facilities abroad," Area Development 12 (May 1977): pp. 58, 60.

13. Alun Morgan and Roger Blanpain, The Industrial Relations and Employment Impacts of Multinational Enterprises (Paris: Organization for Economic Cooperation and Development, 1977), p. 17.

14. Ton Devos, "American Multinationals in Europe and Worker Participation" (Paper presented at the Annual Meeting of the American Political Science Association, September 1976), p. 15.

15. "EEC labor unions gang up on multinationals," World Business Weekly 2 (June 18, 1979): p. 60.

16. "EEC's Plethora of Regs Requires Watching by International Firms," Business International 27 (March 21, 1980): p. 91.

17. Alfred L. Thimm, Recent Trends in German Codetermination Legislation and the Future of Capitalism in Europe, Administrative and Engineering Systems Monograph AES 7701 (Schenectady, N.Y.: Union College and University, January 1977), f.n. 31, p. 6.

18. Ibid., p. 18.

19. Commission on Codetermination, Codetermination in the Enterprise, pp. 2-3.

20. James C. Furlong, Labor in the Boardroom: The Peaceful Revolution (Princeton: Dow Jones Books, 1977), p. 44.

21. Ibid.

22. Alfred L. Thimm, "Decision Making at Volkswagen 1972-1975," Columbia Journal of World Business 11 (Spring 1979): p. 99.

23. Jeremy Bacon and James K. Brown, The Board of Directors: Perspectives and Practices in Nine Countries, Conference Board Report No. 728 (New York: The Conference Board, 1977), p. 37.

24. "Given worker directors' awareness of the realities of the market, investors have had little to fear from their existence. The codetermination industries in Germany have had no problems in acquiring capital and their share values have generally been comparable to those of other sectors. Where this has not been the case the problem has been the general economic state of the industry . . . Despite the original aims of codetermination, it has not led to any control over the growth of economic power . . . More generally, the fact that foreign investment in Germany exceeds German investment abroad . . . indicates that neither German nor foreign investors have felt that the 'dangers' of worker directors seriously compromise the chances of a profitable return." Eric Batstone, "Industrial democracy and worker representation at board level: a review of the European experience," in Industrial Democracy Committee, Industrial Democracy: European Committee (London: Her Majesty's Stationery Office, 1977), p. 37.

25. "Why International Firms Give Germany High Marks as an Investment?" Business International 25 (April 21, 1978): pp. 124-25.

26. Rainer Hellman, Transnational Control of Multinational Corporations (New York: Praeger, 1977), pp. 99-100.

27. Joachim Gabler, University of Frankfurt am Main, "Participation and the Working of the Price Mechanism in a Market Economy," in David F. Heathfield, ed., Economics of Codetermination (London: MacMillan Press, 1977), pp. 55-56.

28. Walter Galenson, School of Industrial and Labor Relations, Cornell University, "Comments," in National Commission for Manpower Policy, Trade and Employment: A Conference Report, Special Report No. 30 (Washington: November 1978), p. 249.

29. Thimm, "Decision Making," p. 94.

30. ". . . it can be further anticipated that top managers will be assessed as much by their ability to get along with the union as much as by their entrepreneurial qualities." Thimm, "Decision Making," p. 102.

31. Thimm, "Recent Trends," p. 4.

32. Sonning Bredemeier, "Lower Saxony: VW means business all round," Business Location File 3, no. 5 (1979): p. 8.

33. UAW Public Relations and Publications Department, "Report of the UAW-VWOA 1978 Tentative Settlement," October 8, 1978.

34. New York Times, International Economic Survey "Car Makers Forging New Alliances," February 3, 1980, sec. 12, p. 17; and "France: The carmakers push for worldwide status," Business Week, no. 2658 (October 13, 1980): p. 57.

35. "Renault to Get Control of AMC under Proposal," Wall Street Journal, September 25, 1980, p. 3.

36. Commission on Codetermination, Codetermination in the Enterprise, part IV, par. 44.

37. Bacon and Brown, Board of Directors, p. 35.

38. Jules Arbose, "Is Worker Democracy Working? Many Experts in Sweden are doubtful," International Management 34 (November 1979): p. 18.

39. Commission on Codetermination, Codetermination in the Enterprise, part IV, par. 68.

40. Commission on Codetermination, Codetermination in the Enterprise, part IV, par. 44.

41. James C. Furlong, "Manager's Journal: Codetermination," Wall Street Journal, March 31, 1980, p. 20.

42. Jean J. Boddewyn, "Divestment, Local vs. Foreign and U.S. vs. European Approaches," Management International Review 19, no. 1 (1979): p. 24.

8

PLANT-CLOSING LEGISLATION:
AN INFLUENCE ON LOCATION

LACK OF PUBLIC POLICY

Government and Management

In the United States, the major public approach to plant closings has not been to deal with the underlying causes of the management decision through industrial and location policy. Rather, assistance is offered to employees and communities after the decision by management has been made. "The United States is notable for the almost total absence of public redundancy policy."[1] Government is not alone in failing to look ahead at the implications of divestment. Until recently, corporate planning has placed far greater emphasis on expansion than on divestment of facilities.[2] As a result, facilities are frequently closed with little advance notice to the affected groups. The enactment of plant-closing legislation would represent a reversal in the responsibilities of government and business. The legislation would indicate acceptance of an additional influence on the location of industry.

Demands for Legislation

On the assumption that plant closings and transfers cause irreparable harm to employees and communities, there have been strong efforts to enact legislation, now before Congress and state legislatures, that would mitigate the adverse effects. With the exception of two "less stringent and loosely enforced"[3] state bills in Maine and Wisconsin, no state or federal legislation has been enacted.

Features of the proposed legislation are that businesses over a certain size or minimum number of employees give advance notice to employees, communities and government agencies of forthcoming closings or shutdowns, moves or major cutbacks in operations. Most proposals also call for severance pay to employees and adjustment payments to communities. The bills do impinge directly on the ability of business to carry out locational decisions; they could temporarily delay the closing of facilities or the moving of operations.

Powerful groups both support and oppose the legislation. "Business interests have stated that the location decision will be affected . . . because of the length of the required notification period and the 'anti-business' disincentive to invest created by the bill."[4] Strong support has not only come from unions but from a variety of social activist organizations, e.g., The Conference on Alternative State and Local Public Policies, and the Ohio Public Interest Campaign.[5] As a United States senator, Walter Mondale was a strong supporter of plant-closing legislation[6] and in 1974 introduced such legislation.[7]

This chapter examines the potential impact of the legislation on the location decisions of business, and legislation's effectiveness in protecting employees and maintaining the economic viability of communities. Existing legislation in Western Europe and Canada, and the U.S. Trade Readjustment Allowance program provide a basis for evaluation.

LEGISLATION IN THE UNITED STATES

Legislation Enacted

Following the closing of Alpha Carbide facilities, the Maine legislation (Title 26 MRSA, Section 625-A) was enacted in 1976 to provide protection for employees. The law covers industrial or commercial facilities employing 100 or more workers in the past year. An employer relocating or terminating an establishment covered by this legislation is liable to his employees for severance pay at the rate of one week's pay for each year of employment. The employer is not liable if: the closing is due to a physical calamity; there is a separate contract for severance pay; an employee accepts employment at a new location; or, the employee has been with the firm less than three years. The intention to close or relocate a facility must be given to the state at least 60 days in advance.

During the first three years after the bill was enacted, no covered firm was liable for severance pay for the following reasons: the company went bankrupt; the business was in operation less than three years; or employees accepted employment at a new location. Bankruptcy is categorized as a physical calamity.[8]

The Wisconsin legislation (Section 109.75) passed in 1975 is directed at mergers, liquidations, disposition, relocations and closings. A corporation with 100 or more employees is required to give 60-days advance notice of such action to affected employees, communities, and the State Department of Labor, Industry and Human Relations. The primary concern of the legislation is to mitigate the impact on employees. Violation of the law by an employer is a misdemeanor, subject to a fine up to $50 for each employee losing a job.

State Bills

The Ohio Community Readjustment Act (SB 188-HB 968), first introduced in 1977, has frequently served as a model for bills which have been introduced in other states. Though there are variations among the state bills, the Ohio bill can be considered a prototype. Compared to the other states, there has been a stronger drive by supporters in Ohio to attain passage.

The Ohio bill contains provisions covering the closing, relocation, and reduction in operations. Any commercial, industrial, or agricultural corporation with 100 or more employees, operating in the state for five years, is subject to the legislation. The basic provisions are for a two-year advance notice, filing of an economic impact statement, severance payments to employees, and payments to communities.

Prenotification must be made to the state, employees, union, and community. Collective bargaining agreements calling for longer notification periods or greater severance pay take precedence. Within 90 days after notification, the firm must prepare an economic impact statement. It must include information on the payroll, number of affected employees, state and local tax revenue to be lost, and the financial effect on other businesses in the community. Severance benefits to employees consist of one payment equal to the average weekly wage times the number of years employed. In lieu of severance benefits, employees who are moving to accept new jobs may select reasonable relocation expenses covering their families and possessions. Health insurance benefits must be continued for six months after the loss of employment. The firm must make payments to the State Community Assistance Fund equal to 10 percent of annual wages of all employees losing their jobs. The fund provides for employment opportunities, for emergency tax relief, and for matching funds to obtain federal assistance. Failure to comply with the statute is a misdemeanor and an employer may be enjoined from closing, relocating, or reducing operations until proper notice has been given. There is no indication how an employer could actually be enjoined from such action, nor is there any mention of how the liability of financially ailing firms for payments would be covered.

Federal Bills

A state enacting plant-closing legislation would be handicapped in retaining or attracting industry when other states have no comparable legislation. The effectiveness of any state legislation would be vitiated by the ability of companies that do not comply to take the costs of closing or relocating a facility as a federal tax deduction. Federal legislation would preempt the state bills and clarify the interstate situation. It would prevent a company that does not comply from offsetting the closing costs against taxes.

In 1980, two key bills on plant closings were before Congress, HR5040/S1608, the National Employment Priorities Act of 1979, sponsored by Representative William Ford and Senator Donald Riegle both of Michigan, and S1609, the Employee Protection and Community Stabilization Act of 1979, sponsored by Senator Harrison Williams of New Jersey. After scheduled hearings one bill was expected to emerge. Chances of immediate passage were considered slim by the sponsors; however, they anticipated growing support which would subsequently lead to passage. The advent of the Reagan administration dimmed the legislative outlook and unions shifted to collective bargaining for protection from plant closings.[9]

There are differences in the bills. The coverage of S1609 extends to plant closings or transfers in manufacturing, mining, transportation, and wholesaling establishments with 50 or more employees. Executive, administrative and professional personnel are excluded. Prenotification of one year is required. Thirty days later an economic impact statement must be filed. Severance pay consists of 85 percent of weekly pay for a year (including unemployment insurance). Employees over 55 years of age receive another year of benefits. The employees' purchase of facilities is stressed. Employees have rights to employment at the location to which the facilities were transferred, relocation allowances, and maintenance of health and welfare benefits for a year. The affected community is entitled to 100 percent of one year's tax loss. Penalties for not complying, e.g., prenotification and severance payments, are the loss of federal tax deductions for the costs of terminating or transferring the facilities. If the firm fails to make the payments to employees, the government assumes the liability, and holds the firm liable. Nothing is specifically mentioned about bankrupt or insolvent firms unless it is implied that the government will meet the financial obligations. There is no specific mention about failure to make the payments to communities.

S1608 covers firms with an annual gross sales volume or business of at least $250,000 with a minimum of 50 employees in a factory, plant, mine, business office, or other single working place. The change must affect either 15 percent of the employees, or 100 employees. The prenotification period varies; for 500 or more employees, it is 2 years; for 100 to 500 employees, it is 18 months; and for less than 100 employees, it is 6 months. Severance pay is calculated at 85 percent of weekly pay for a year, including unemployment insurance and trade adjustment allowances. The maximum payment is $25,000. Employees 53 to 61 years of age receive additional coverage.

The government could provide financial and technical assistance that contributes to the economic viability of covered firms. Assistance for the employees' purchase of facilities in this bill is not as detailed as in S1609. Payment to communities is 85 percent of annual tax revenues lost. If the firm fails to make payment to employees or the community, the government does so, and holds the firm liable. When a firm transfers overseas, the mandated payment to communities is 300 percent of annual tax revenues lost. Violations subject the firm to the imposition of civil penalties equal to certain tax deductions.

FUNCTIONING PROGRAMS

Trade Adjustment Assistance

There are a number of domestic and foreign functioning programs, which vary somewhat from the federal and state bills, but still have sufficient commonality to serve as a guide to policy formulation. [10] In the United States, a body of experience for evaluating the plant-closing legislation emanates from the trade adjustment assistance program. It was designed to assist workers and firms adversely affected by increases in imports and changed competitive conditions. The program was started under the Trade Expansion Act of 1962 (TEA) (PL 87-794). There was recognition that import-related problems do not have to be industry-wide but may involve individual firms and groups of workers. Congress decided that the federal government should assume a special responsibility to domestic firms because of the policies designed to encourage foreign trade. Workers, firms and communities should be given assistance beyond the existing state unemployment insurance or government business assistance programs.

There have been differing expectations on what the assistance could accomplish. Assistance could be used to keep firms open within the same industry; or, it could not only keep such firms open, but could facilitate their shift to a new industry in which they would become competitive. [11]

The Trade Act of 1974 (PL 93-618) liberalized the 1962 Trade Expansion Act. Under the new Act, the U. S. Labor Department certifies eligibility for assistance. State agencies deliver benefits to workers in the form of a weekly cash trade readjustment allowance added to unemployment insurance, and employment and relocation services. The U. S. Department of Commerce administers the assistance for firms and communities.

Workers can qualify for weekly trade adjustment allowances equal to 70 percent of their average weekly wage minus any unemployment insurance benefits. The proceeds cannot exceed the national average weekly manufacturing wage. The allowance may be received for up to a year with an additional 26 weeks available to those in approved training programs, and to those 60 years of age or more on the separation date. There are no provisions for maintenance of medical benefits, seniority or pension rights. State unemployment insurance officials feel there should be no difference in the treatment of any recipient of unemployment insurance and adjustment benefits. [12]

The use of benefits under trade adjustment assistance is somewhat different than it is likely to be under the plant-closing legislation. Most workers under trade adjustment assistance await recall rather than accept other jobs. Few take advantage of the aids for training, job search or job relocation. Other firms offering lower wages or benefits are reluctant to hire laid-off workers fearing they would return to their former jobs if recalled;[13] however, this attitude might be short-sighted. National and local union officials assert that trade adjustment assistance is only a temporary remedy and does nothing to solve the complex problems of job loss due to imports. The workers are helped for a limited period but "generally, workers are not placed in new employment and ultimately might be unemployed."[14]

Firms impacted by imports can be helped with government loans up to $1 million, 90 percent guarantee of private bank loans up to $3 million, technical assistance, and 75 percent of the costs of technical assistance provided by private consultants. Firms that provide component parts, services, or suppliers related to manufacture of the impacted product are likely to be ineligible for assistance. For example, a firm producing yarn used in sweaters was ineligible because imports of the end product, sweaters, and not imports of yarn were increasing. The yarn firm petitioned for assistance but was refused since it did not produce sweaters. [15] This case indicates a potential problem area for plant-closing legislation in determining how far linkages from the primary impacted firm should extend to other affected firms. The legislation will have to consider if employees and communities not directly related to the impacted firm are entitled to benefits. Another difficult facet of state legislation would be the ramifications when a firm operates in several states.

The General Accounting Office found that firms in the trade adjustment assistance program are generally in such poor financial condition when they receive benefits that the loans are not large enough to make any appreciable difference in the firm's financial condition. Most firms do not use the proceeds to improve their competitive position. The loan proceeds are often utilized to pay debts or for working capital rather than to modernize plant and equipment, improve production, or make product changes. The amount of the loans is not sufficient to enable a firm to make all of the necessary improvements. [16]

The Department of Commerce has followed a policy of encouraging trade-impacted communities to use existing Commerce programs. The General Accounting Office found that trade-impacted communities have had to compete for limited federal funds with communities having economic problems attributable to other factors. The Department of Commerce agreed that more could be done to identify and assist trade-impacted communities; but because of budgetary constraints and the availability of other economic adjustment programs, these communities should not be given special preference. Imports are only one cause of economic dislocation and the limited funds should go to areas of greatest need regardless of the cause. The Department of Commerce has raised the point that communities face a nearly impossible task to develop data that would establish their eligibility under the Trade Act criteria. [17]

Like assistance to firms, there is a question concerning the extent communities with the limited assistance can make sufficient changes to attain economic viability. Will the aid be allocated for subsidies, promotion, recruiting campaigns, or for the improvement of infrastructure, services? Another viewpoint asserts that it may be necessary to withhold aid from communities that have little likelihood of becoming viable.

An unfavorable sign for plant-closing legislation is that "the adjustment assistance provisions of the Trade Expansion Act have generally been conceded to be a failure."[18] This is a judgment shared by unions, companies and administrators of the program. Reasons for failure could be summarized by "labor's oft repeated comment that adjustment assistance is essentially burial assistance."[19]

A basic problem of the trade adjustment assistance and the plant-closing legislation is that by the time calamity strikes and corrective action is taken too much time has already elapsed. The disintegration of a firm or industry takes place regardless of formal prenotification requirements. A preventive approach should focus on identifying emerging problem areas and seek remedies at an early stage.[20] Yet, the availability of benefits should not be foreclosed.

Canada

The Canadian programs have particular relevance for the United States because Canada has multiple systems, federal, provincial and territorial (Yukon and Northwest) with differing requirements. (See Table 8.1.) Judicial interpretation has given provincial legislatures

TABLE 8.1

Canadian Prenotification Requirements

Juris-diction	Employees involved in the layoff	Minimum layoff period	Workers laid off	Length of prenotifi-cation
Federal	50 or more*		50–100	8 weeks
			101–300	12 weeks
			over 300	16 weeks
Manitoba	50 or more		see Federal	see Federal
Ontario	50 or more	13 weeks	50–199	8 weeks
			200–499	12 weeks
			500 or more	16 weeks
Quebec	10 or more	6 months	10–100	2 months
			101–300	3 months
			over 300	4 months
Newfoundland			to 199	8 weeks
			200–499	12 weeks
			500 or more	16 weeks
Nova Scotia	10 or more		see Quebec	see Quebec

Source: U. S. General Accounting Office, Considerations For Adjustment Assistance Under the 1974 Trade Act: A Summary of Techniques Used in Other Countries, Volume II: Profiles of Adjustment Programs in Eight Countries, ID-78-43 (Washington, D. C. , Jan. 18, 1979), p. 45; and Labour Canada, Report of the Commission of Inquiry into Redundancies and Lay-Offs (Ottawa, March 1979), pp. 146-147.
*Includes supervisory and managerial personnel.

major jurisdiction over labor matters with a limited role assigned to
the federal government. About 400,000 workers come under federal
jurisdiction. [21] Notice of group termination is given to the affected
employees, Minister of Labor of the designated jurisdiction and, in
certain instances, to a certified trade union. Only the federal jurisdiction makes severance payments a statutory right; the Labor Code
(Part III: S61 p. 302) provides for two days pay for each year of continuous service after five years of employment. The amount is not
considered sufficient to be considered income replacement.

> . . . in the area of manpower policy [including collective
> dismissals] the otherwise strict delineation between the
> powers of the Federal government and those of the prov-
> inces in labor matters does not fully apply. [22]

Western Europe

Programs have been operational for many years in Western
Europe with the objective of mitigating the severe effects of plant
closings and the ensuing economic dislocation. Legal protection for
the victims of layoffs is deemed a necessary component of social policy even at the cost of efficiency, e.g. delays in establishing operations at the optimum plant location. This view could be the outcome
of a long-standing belief that job insecurity has a direct correlation
with social unrest which increases geometrically with a lack of mean-
ingful employment.

The increasingly stringent conditions placed on employers by
European laws on dismissals reflect the philosophy that "it is prefer-
able from the point of view of the national economy to keep workers
in employment even if this increases the cost to the individual employer."[23] Yet, there is recognition in Western Europe that the process
of economic growth has to continue simultaneously with concern for
workers.

> . . . European policy makers believe that economic growth
> and technical change should not take place over the delete-
> rious effects of these processes on working people. Policy
> makers in Europe recognize that while economic growth is
> essential to the well being of the nation, the impact of the
> severe economic dislocations that are often byproducts of
> this process should be reduced. . . . However, in general
> the role of the public sector in Western Europe can be char-
> acterized as one of not standing by and allowing these dis-
> locations to work themselves out through faith in the equi-

librium process of the market. Rather, the public sector has attempted to provide the laws, regulations and programs so that the needs of working people are cared for while the economic growth process continues. [24]

If the United States is nearing the status of a mature economy, then the intensity of demands for job security, special compensation for layoffs, and delays in plant closing and movement along European lines is bound to accelerate.

> In Europe the view is more commonly held that legal protection of workers against lay-offs is a necessary component of national policy, even at the cost of efficiency. European opinion might be a result of a view that job insecurity has a direct correlation with social unrest and that such unrest increases geometrically with a lack of meaningful employment. In a constantly growing economy such as that which North America has enjoyed in the last 40 years, this view of history is usually ignored. Much injustice can be tolerated if an individual believes that, economically at least, things are always going to get better.[25]

Great Britain

The proprietary rights principle is the basis for the British statutory redundancy policy; it holds that a job represents economic and social value, and when tenure is arbitrarily removed, the worker should be compensated accordingly. The main thrust is to compensate the worker for the job loss in cash and then leave him to his own devices. [26] Usually the employer feels that his responsibility ends with the payment, and any subsequent job assistance to the workers is a rare occurrence. [27]

The payments also signify an awareness that certain industries must phase out obsolete facilities and prepare for retrenchment. "In effect, it is a payoff for the unions' acceptance or consent to a rationalization plan and is a compensation consequence of such a position. . . . The redundancy pay program reflects the recognition that workers who sustain permanent job loss were not adequately assisted by the unemployment compensation system."[28] Unemployment compensation is concerned with temporary layoffs and not with permanent unemployment.

Workers in Great Britain are protected by the Employment Protection Act of 1975 and the British Redundancy Payments Act of 1965. A company proposing to lay off 100 or more employees must notify the

unions and the government three months in advance; for layoffs of 10
to 100 workers the notification period is 60 days. A failure to provide
adequate notice is likely to result in workers receiving additional severance pay calculated on the basis of one day's wages for each day's
delay. The only way companies can avoid compliance with the prenotification requirement is to persuade the government that jobs would
be saved by keeping the layoffs secret.[29]

Mandated severance pay comes to a maximum of about $7,500
which is customarily the starting point for bargaining. [30] Unions have
been able to insure that most companies exceed the statutory sum;
some employers double or triple the statutory figure. Workers between 21 and 64 years of age with 2 or more years of service are entitled to severance payments from employers of 1.5 weeks pay per
year of service. This is in addition to the weekly statutory unemployment benefits.

There is a national insurance fund administered by the Ministry
of Labor. Employers can claim a 41 percent rebate on severance payments from the fund. In the event of bankruptcy or employer malfea-
sance, workers are paid by the government which then seeks to re-
cover from the company. Of the 230,000 employees who received
payments in 1978, averaging about £740, 15 percent had to be paid
entirely from the fund. [31] The power to withhold the 41 percent as a
penalty engenders compliance from employers.

France

A key feature of French industrial relations law is a high degree
of state intervention. Working conditions are regulated in considerable
detail not only legally but also by national agreements between the Confederation of Employers and the central union federations. These agreements are then adopted in industry-wide agreements that receive the
force of law through ministerial decrees.

The involvement in industrial relations extends to plant closings.
"French law has progressively given the government and unions the
right to delay and modify a company's decision to reduce the number
of available jobs. "[32] Permission to reduce the number of employees
can be denied by the government if dismissals are based on other than
economic criteria, e.g. to avoid compliance with a collective bargaining agreement. The French Supreme Court has ruled that:

> The employer . . . is the only judge of the circumstances
> that induce him to go out of business and there is no legal
> provision obliging him to remain in business merely to in-
> sure stability of employment for his staff. [33]

In practice unemployment has become such a sensitive issue that French employers are reluctant to lay off employees and thus provoke industrial unrest and "they also find it increasingly difficult to obtain official approval for such layoffs. "[34]

> There are specified procedures covering the dismissals of ten or more employees in a thirty day period. Employee representatives and the government must be given all pertinent information including measures being taken to avoid or limit the number of dismissals. To forestall employees from being presented with unexpected dismissal notices, French law gives the employee representatives the right to examine developments relative to employment within the enterprise over the past year and to be informed of the firm's future policies. The firm is obligated to formulate a "regulement interieur" which is part of the employment contract and specifies the procedures to be taken in the event of redundancies. [35]

Severance pay is mandated by ministerial decree. All employees with at least two years of continuous service with the same employer are entitled. The minimum amount of severance pay is equal to ten hours wages or one-twentieth of a month's salary calculated on the basis of the worker's annual earnings during the preceding three months. [36]

The Netherlands

The arrangements in the Netherlands are patterned after the West German system. Layoffs other than those agreed to by labor and management must be approved by a district employment office. For layoffs of 20 or more employees, a three-month notification period is mandated; this is considered an opportunity for programs or plans to be negotiated to save jobs or relocate workers. There is no fixed amount set for severance pay; rather, it is an amount negotiated by employers and unions. Shop workers usually receive six months pay and it is not rare for salaried workers to receive up to two years pay.

Neither the Western Germans nor the Dutch will allow mass layoffs unless there is a social plan to protect workers. The rationalization of production is not considered a sufficient motive. "The restructuring must be intended to keep the company from going bust. "[37] This attitude is exemplified by the plans of the British tobacco conglomerate, BAT industries, to close an obsolete Dutch factory. The closing was halted by the Dutch courts despite BAT's assertion that is was losing money on the factory; the company was ordered to reopen negotiations with the Dutch trade unions. An outside expert hired by the court to determine if the closing was mandated by economic necessity concluded that the Dutch and Belgian plants of BAT should be considered one economic unit. "The implications for other multinationals wishing to close single, uneconomic plants are not hard to imagine."[38] Such decisions have the effect of removing corporate mobility and increasing the desirability of the United States as a site for operations.

Sweden

Employers are obligated to give advance notice to the union, county branch of the labor market board, and to individual employees being dismissed before closing a plant or reducing the level of employment permanently. The length of advance notice depends on the number of employees involved: for less than 25, it is 2 months; for 25 to 200, it is four months; and for over 100, it is six months.

Before implementing the cutbacks, the employer must await the results of negotiations with the union. If an agreement cannot be reached, labor court approval is the only remaining constraint.

When the county branch receives notice of the closing or cutback, consultation may take place among representatives of the labor board, employer, employees, and local government to facilitate readjustment. The main task is to assist in the selection of measures: other employment by existing or new firms in the area; training to acquire new skills; waiting until production returns to normal or new jobs are available; or creating public relief-employment.

There is no statutory obligation for employers to make severance payments. An agreement in 1974 between the Swedish Employers Federation (SAF) and the Trade Union Federation (LO) created a central fund. The member firms of SAF contribute 0.1 percent of their annual payroll. The fund is administered by a jointly created insurance institute. The fund's resources are not intended for use as a general severance pay system, but rather to assist older workers with long service who become redundant. Their right to severance pay exists for five years; and if new employment ends within that period, the worker can still claim payment from the fund.[39] Though the closing decision must be negotiated with the union, the final power still rests with the company:

> While there are conflicting interpretations, it appears that
> none of this has fundamentally affected the decision-making
> power of corporations to reduce, close or relocate opera-

tions based on profit and-loss criteria—to the dismay of some trade union militants. Ordinarily the most the government can do, if a company is insistent on shutting down, is to affect the _timing_ of that decision and to place certain very important constraints on the way it is implemented. In the process, a much greater share of the "social costs" of the shutdown, which in the U. S. would be forced upon affected workers and communities, are absorbed by the corporation and the government in Sweden.[40]

West Germany

West German companies with more than 20 employees are required to give the works council elected by the workers notice prior to the implementation of any critical decisions, including layoffs. The reasons for dismissals or layoffs as well as access to corporate data must be given. A social plan has to be negotiated by the employer and the works council; it normally includes the selection of workers to be laid off, the effective date of the action, and the amount of severance pay. If there is no agreement on a social plan, the final arbiter on the timing of the layoffs is the Regional Labor Department. Notification is required if 25 or more workers, or 10 percent of a work force of 60 or more, are to be dismissed within 30 days.

The government does not dictate to the company what the workers should be given as severance pay.[41] However, the social plan usually has provisions for severance pay. The trend in recent years has been for employers to persuade workers to leave voluntarily by offering a higher separation pay than could be obtained under a social plan. Employers prefer this approach since it minimizes the need to follow the complex procedures required with collective dismissals. Younger workers find this especially attractive since their payments are not based on length of service.[42] In the event of bankruptcy, workers are entitled to three months salary, but if company assets are inadequate, the government makes the payment.

Some companies stretch out the dismissal notices by laying off small numbers of workers to avoid compliance with the prenotification requirement. Employers and unions differ on the impact of the legislation. Employers claim that the cost of dismissing workers is responsible for the sluggish rate of job creation. Employers are aware of the heavy costs entailed in reducing employment and are therefore reluctant to hire additional workers. Trade unionists assert that employers neglect and misuse the legislation by failing to comply until they are forced to by works councils and unions. Penalties under the law are minimal and enforcement is lax; in the end the employer decides. "Moreover, the works councils cannot influence the overall economy—only local management decisions. They cannot cope with problems arising from restructuring and rapid technological change."[43]

EVALUATION OF PLANT-CLOSING LEGISLATION

Prenotification

The desirable length of the prenotification period is debatable.[44] The earlier the notice is received, the better the opportunity is to devise and take remedial measures. Employees can seek out new jobs. Communities can seek replacement industries or arrange for the takeover of vacated facilities. The government, labor and industry can devise alternative plans.

The proposed legislation in the United States calls for a prenotification period generally of one or two years which is appreciably longer than the periods in other countries. Too long an interval can lead to a deterioration of industrial and community relations, poor employee morale and departure of key employees, including managerial. A protracted notification period can make workers and their families vulnerable to psychosomatic distress if no solution appears imminent.[45] Prenotification could reveal corporate strategy to competitors through the filing of economic impact statements. Competitors will have an incentive to invade local markets, i.e. those serviced from the closed facilities. Prenotification could cause problems by making finance sources wary of extending credit to firms that are reducing operations or closing facilities. There is the danger that public awareness of a troubled facility could compound the company's difficulties.

It is not always possible to have a long prenotification period. "Today's international business environment is so charged with uncertainty that a once profitable plant or subsidiary can turn into a loss ridden burden all too unexpectedly."[46] A two-year period for a firm like Chrysler is impractical when there is so much doubt about its survival which depends on external factors such as government help.

The requirement for advance notice is paralleled by legislation in many states designed to regulate takeovers of corporations organized or operated within their jurisdiction. The purpose is to protect target companies by giving them time to respond to takeover efforts. The protection does not have to apply only to target companies and stockholders but could extend to employees and communities. A corporation generally seeking takeover of another company must give notice of its intention accompanied by information about itself and the corporate plans for the company it wants. Then there is a waiting period before the takeover bid can proceed.

The Ohio takeover legislation requires that a corporation seeking another business submits "a statement of any plans or proposal which the offerer, upon gaining control, may have to liquidate the target company, sell its assets, effect a merger or consolidation of it, or make any other major change in its business, corporate structure, management personnel, or policies or employment."[47] The similarity in the takeover and plant-closing legislation suggests that the two should be coordinated.

Severance Payments

The availability of severance payments can ease resistance to closings, make employees more amenable to retraining or relocating, and give management more flexibility to close plants. On the other hand, a high level of severance payments encourages the substitution of capital for labor and the reluctance to hire workers.

Severance pay affects the attitude of workers toward retention of their jobs. With offers of sizable redundancy (severance) pay, the resolve of workers in the United Kingdom to see that plants are kept open collapses. Subsequently, workers find that their severance pay does not last as long as anticipated; by then, it is too late. Furthermore, redundancy pay does nothing to create jobs for workers entering the labor force in affected communities. Some shop stewards attempt to convince workers that the jobs are not theirs to sell and that they should resist the temptation to accept the payments on the assumption that somehow the government or union can keep the plants open.[48] "Negotiations crumble out of union control as men grab the money and dream of running their own tobacconist jobs."[49] Generous and immediate money offers distract workers from efforts to stop closure or at least to improve the terms. The employers get out of a bad situation and the unions lose members. Concurrently, the community's efforts to keep the plant in operation are undermined.

Another approach to minimizing the cost of laying off employees is to maintain or create jobs. France's major chemical fibers company, Rhone-Poulenc, persuaded a dozen companies to provide jobs for its workers near the plants it intended to close. Rhone-Poulenc sold a factory at Besancon to the medical equipment manufacturer, Informatek, at a bargain price and offered production and sales assistance on condition that 100 jobs were created for the laid-off Rhone-Poulenc workers.[50]

The potential shutdown could be a hidden and growing contingent liability. Enka, a subsidiary of the Dutch chemical company, Akso,

estimates that each laid-off employee costs the company $15,000.[51]
A rough estimate of termination liabilities of typical manufacturing
subsidiaries based on simulated shutdowns indicated costs as high as
150 percent of annual payroll in parts of Europe. Termination payments at the upper-management levels are greater than at the blue-
and white-collar levels in a number of countries, e. g. Belgium, Italy,
Japan, and Spain; payments for senior managers can add up to 250
percent or more of annual cash income.[52]

There is a strong likelihood that a plant closing will be accompanied by bankruptcy or the inability of firms to meet their mandated
obligations, especially for severance pay. A number of governments
have plans to assume the costs of severance payments when firms
are unable to meet their obligations.[53] By excluding new firms with
their high rate of failure, the incidence of bankruptcy or nonpayment
can be minimized.[54]

Funding Severance Payments

There are insurance funds to guarantee that laid-off workers
will receive severance payments. The nine Common Market countries
have approved a measure that extends protection to workers in bankrupt companies. Workers are assured that either the company or the
government would honor commitments for severance pay, pensions,
seniority, medical and other benefits. Previously workers in a number of EEC countries received severance pay only after the firm's
creditors had been satisfied and had lost all their accumulated rights.
This void would be filled by the agreement of the Ministers for Employment and Social Affairs to set up a mechanism to guarantee the
unpaid claims of workers in an insolvent firm. Under the new system,
which is scheduled to be operational by 1982, each government would
establish an institution to guarantee the payment of employee claims
in the event of insolvency. There would be a ceiling on payments. Employers would have to contribute to the guarantee institution in each
country unless the government decided to use public funds.

To forestall concerns about the ability of firms to make payments when dismissals are imminent, consideration should be given
to establishing a fund before a crisis arrives. Otherwise, firms going
bankrupt might be unable to meet the heavy financial obligations for
payments to employees and communities. The establishment of funds
to which contributions are made periodically would allow firms to
make reasonable payments so that facilities could be closed with a
minimum of bitterness. Workers would not be so resistant to structural and technological change, and relocation to optimum locations
would be facilitated. Assets of the funds could be used for short-term
industrial development loans.

Industry-wide redundancy funds have been proposed in Canada, at least for certain industries, to ease the hardships on workers losing their jobs. They would supplement existing income maintenance programs such as unemployment insurance. However, a government-appointed commission, while not objecting in principle to this proposal, strongly suggested that the primary effort should be directed toward finding alternate employment. The effort required to set up and operate an industry-wide fund might better be devoted to the establishment of a permanent joint industry-wide manpower committee of labor and management under the auspices of the Canada Manpower Consultative Service into which a supplementary unemployment benefit plan might be incorporated. [55]

Alternatives that could be applicable are severance taxes or mandatory contributions. For example, the European Coal and Steel Community places a levy on the production of coal and steel; since 1972, the rate has been 0.29 percent. Among the beneficiaries are redundant workers.

A number of states have placed severance taxes on minerals and other natural resources; however, there are no allocations for worker benefits. Another model could be the programs operational in various European countries, notably France, which mandate employers to allocate a fixed percentage of salaries and wages to housing; the employer has the option of participating either alone or with other firms. [56] It would be desirable if employees' severance payments could be recycled back into regional economic development without the complications of employee ownership. [57]

Employer and Employee Coverage

The proposed state and federal bills omit coverage for large groups of employers and employees. The requirement that only firms with a minimum number of employees have to comply gives small firms a flexibility or freedom that large firms are denied, e.g. to close or relocate a plant without incurring heavy costs. The workers in small firms are denied the benefits that workers in large firms can receive.

The Conservative government in Britain has decided that it is wrong to create "a second tier of employees who have less protection, especially since protection is no less necessary in small firms than in large. The longer that employment protection continues in large firms, the more workers in small firms will regard exemption for their employers as an unwarranted denial of a basic legal right."[58]

Initially unemployment insurance benefits in the United States were available only to employees of firms with 20 or more workers;

TABLE 8.2

Unemployment Insurance Coverage of Employees
in the United States

	Percentage		
	1939	1960	1973
Agriculture	—	8.1	25.7
Manufacturing	94.7	99.2	100.0
Services	49.0	54.5	88.8
State & Local Government	—	5.8	25.2

Source: Robert J. Rossana, "Unemployment Insurance Programs: A New Look for the Eighties," Business Review Federal Re-
serve Bank of Philadelphia (July/August 1979): p. 20.

however, most employees are now covered, and there could be a similar progression with the plant-closing legislation. (See Table 8.2.)

Another group excluded from most bills are employees of government or nonprofit organizations. Yet, government employees in
particular are becoming increasingly subject to layoffs and the closing
of facilities; as indicated in Table 8.2, they are increasingly obtaining
unemployment insurance benefits.

Despite the wording in the various bills and the persistent refer-
ence to plant closings, the applicability reaches beyond plants, and
the impact would extend beyond the manufacturing sector.

Effect on Location

There are contradictory claims on the effects of the plant-
closing legislation on locational decisions of industry. Proponents of
the legislation assert that limits on plant closings will not deter management from selecting areas with regulations, e.g. West Germany.

Regulation of plant movement does not automatically stran-
gle economic growth or result in massive stagnation of economic systems, as business interests charge. Indeed, many
of the countries with the most stringent restrictions, such
as West Germany, are also those with the highest growth
rates and the lowest unemployment figures in the 1970s.
The U.S. corporations that react angrily to proposals for

limits on unfettered capital mobility often are the very same corporations that manage to live reasonably comfortably with those regulations in countries where they have foreign subsidiaries. [59]

On the other hand, there is the assertion that one of the major attractions for foreign direct investment is the flexibility in laying off workers and the resultant lowered fixed costs. According to the American Productivity Center, labor in the United States has priced itself into the world labor market by settling for moderate wage increases and not insisting on as much job security as European workers. "American corporations . . . continue to have, by European standards, an extraordinary freedom to lay off workers when orders shrink. So they fret less about the risk of a labor surplus (a flexible cost) than a capital surplus (a fixed cost)."[60]

The United States is depicted as a location where large-scale reorganizations can be accomplished without long disputes with employees, unions, and local community leaders. The ability to streamline a company is considered a major factor in the surge of U.S. investment by European chemical companies. [61]

Effect on Industrial Development

The plant-closing costs imposed by legislation could deter expansions or construction of new facilities by making alternative and more productive locations overly expensive. "Restrictions on business mobility will increase production costs by reducing the efficiency with which resources are allocated on an inter and intraregional basis."[62] In the cost calculus for plant-closing legislation, the imposition of a price for discontinuing operations and some loss of foreign direct investment[63] must be balanced against the potential long-range savings to management and the nation from the closing of outmoded and inefficient facilities. The implementation of a national industrial policy cannot take place without a drastic restructuring but, it is mandatory that the hardships to the affected groups caused by the restructuring be mitigated. If the private sector is unable to absorb the costs then, the public sector must be a contributor. Otherwise the industrial development of the United States will continue to lag in a competitive world economy.

NOTES

1. Canada, Minister of Labor, Report of the Commission of Inquiry on Redundancies and Lay-Offs (Ottawa: Labor Canada, March 1979), p. 183.

2. Yoshi Tsurumi, The Japanese Are Coming: A Multinational Interaction of Firms and Politics (Cambridge, Mass.: Ballinger Publishing, 1976), pp. 214-15.

3. "An American Exit Tax," Wall Street Journal, December 7, 1978, p. 20.

4. C&R Associates, Plant Closing Legislation and Regulation in the United States and Western Europe: A Survey, prepared for the Federal Trade Commission under Contract L0458 (January 1979), p. 46.

5. For background on these organizations see Neal R. Pierce and Jerry Hagstrom, "Watch Out, New Right, Here Come the Young Progressives," National Journal 10 (December 30, 1979): p. 2071; and David Osborne, "Renegade Tax Reform: Turning Prop 13 on Its Head," Saturday Review (May 12, 1979): p. 20.

6. U.S., Congress, House of Representatives, Committee on Education and Labor, General Subcommittee on Labor, The National Employment Priorities Act: Hearings on H.R. 13541, 93rd Cong., 2d sess., 1974.

7. Albert H. Jaeggin, "Your Company's Life Is at Stake," Area Development 14 (November 1979): p. 4.

8. Letter, Marvin W. Ewing, Director, Bureau of Labor, Department of Manpower Affairs, State of Maine, April 6, 1979.

9. "Tough Talks Loom, as Unions Shift Focus from Congress to Contracts," Wall Street Journal, Dec. 30, 1980, p. 1.

10. On the value of comparative studies for policy formulation see Morris L. Sweet and S. George Walters, Mandatory Housing Finance Programs: A Comparative International Analysis (New York: Praeger, 1976), pp. 6-8.

11. U.S., General Accounting Office, Considerations for Adjustment Assistance Under The 1974 Act: A Summary Of Techniques Used In Other Countries, vol. 1, ID-78-43 (January 18, 1979), p. 43.

12. U.S., General Accounting Office, Worker Adjustment Assistance Under The Trade Act Of 1974 To New England Workers Has Been Primarily Income Maintenance, HRD-78-153 (October 31, 1978), p. 21.

13. U.S., General Accounting Office, Worker Adjustment Assistance Under The Trade Act of 1974— Problems In Assisting Auto Workers, HRD-77-152 (January 11, 1978), p. 6.

14. General Accounting Office, Worker Adjustment Assistance, HRD-78-153, p. 22.

15. U.S., General Accounting Office, Adjustment Assistance to

Firms Under The Trade Act Of 1974—Income Maintenance Or Successful Adjustment?, ID-78-53 (December 21, 1978), p. 24.

16. Ibid. , p. 27.

17. General Accounting Office, Considerations for Adjustment vol. 1, ID-78-43, p. 46.

18. U. S. , Congress, Joint Economic Committee, Anticipating Disruptive Imports, 95th Cong. , 2d sess. , 1978, p. 2.

19. Ibid.

20. An example of a preventive approach or early warning approach is presented in U. S. , Congress, Joint Economic Committee, Anticipating Disruptive Imports.

21. The Labor Code, the key federal legislation on labor, applies to: undertakings that connect a province with another province or country; air transport, aircraft and aerodromes; radio and television broadcasting; banks; the defined operations of specific works deemed to be for the general advantage of Canada or two or more provinces; most Federal Crown Corporations, e. g. Canadian Broadcasting Corporation and the St. Lawrence Seaway Authority. Letter, Nicole Marchund, chief, Legislative Analysis, Labour Canada, October 17, 1979.

22. Canada, Minister of Labor, Redundancies and Lay-Offs, p. 124.

23. Canada, Minister of Labor, Redundancies and Lay-Offs, p. 132.

24. C&R Associates, Legislation in Western Europe on Mass Dismissals and Plant Closings: A Review of Studies and Commentaries, with Policy Implications for the United States, prepared for the Federal Trade Commission under Contract L0458 (February 1979), pp. 46-47.

25. Canada, Minister of Labor, Redundancies and Lay-Offs, pp. 36-37.

26. Canada, Minister of Labor, Redundancies and Lay-Offs, p. 106.

27. "The acceptance of responsibility by a departing employer is not unique. . . . But it is rare. " The willingness of the Massey Ferguson company to close a plant in Scotland, make redundancy payments, and look for replacement work for the plant and its employees was a surprising departure from the traditional policy of a company "paying the redundancy money and walking out. " "Massey Ferguson New businesses apply here," Economist 273 (November 24, 1979): pp. 100-1.

28. Joint Report of Labor Union Study Tour Participants, Economic Dislocation, Plant Closings, Plant Relocations and Plant Conversion (May 1, 1979), p. 27.

29. "How layoff rules tie the managers' hands," World Business Weekly 2 (September 24, 1979): p. 11.

30. The nationalized British Steel Corporation workers in the Corby plant were scheduled to receive up to £20,000 in severance pay. The town development corporation hoped to persuade the workers to use their redundancy money to support new companies. "Unemployment New and old," Economist 273 (November 10, 1979): p. 40.

31. "The easier way out," Economist 272 (August 18, 1979): p. 78.

32. C&R Associates, Plant Closing Legislation, p. 37.

33. C&R Associates, Plant Closing Legislation, p. 38.

34. "Unemployed to the left," World Business Weekly 2 (April 21, 1979): p. 40.

35. Canada, Minister of Labor, Redundancies and Lay-Offs, p. 138.

36. Canada, Minister of Labor, Redundancies and Lay-Offs, p. 153.

37. "How Layoff rules tie the managers' hands," World Business Weekly 2 (September 24, 1979).

38. "How Layoff rules tie the managers' hands," World Business Weekly 2 (September 24, 1979).

39. Canada, Minister of Labor, Redundancies and Lay-Offs, p. 156.

40. Joint Report of Labor Union Study Tour Participants, Economic Dislocation, p. 19.

41. "How Layoff rules tie the managers' hands," World Business Weekly 2 (September 24, 1979): p. 11.

42. Canada, Minister of Labor, Redundancies and Lay-Offs, p. 155.

43. Joint Report of Labor Union Study Tour Participants, Economic Dislocation, pp. 22, 26.

44. A May 1980 survey of public affairs and public relations executives of the Fortune 500 companies on advance plant-closing notice elicited 105 responses. Over a third of the respondents considered six months to a year to be the ideal period; 27 percent, three to six months; and 21 percent, two to three months. Fifty-three percent thought a realistic advance notice period to a community would be two to six months. Regarding the one- to two-year period in much of the proposed legislation, 74 percent thought their companies could not reasonably meet this requirement; 14 percent were unsure; 12 percent were confident their companies could meet such a requirement. Reasons cited by top management for not providing advance notice of a plant closing were ranked in order of importance: 51 percent, potential loss of worker productivity; 25 percent, loss of potential business; 6 percent, employee morale; and 3 percent, stock market considerations. "How Much Advance Notice Before Closing A Plant?," Corporate Issues Monitor: A Quarterly Survey of Communications Executives (Peter Small and Associates), July 15, 1980.

45. C&R Associates, Community Costs of Plant Closings: Bibliography and Survey of the Literature, prepared for the Federal Trade Commission under Contract L0362 (July 1978), p. 57.

46. "Multinational companies need strategies for managing termination liabilities,: TPF&C International Letter (Spring/Summer 1977) in Ed Kelly and Lee Webb, eds., Plant Closings: Resources for Public Officials and Activists (Washington, D. C.: Conference on State and Local Policies, May 1979), p. 45.

47. Edward Kelly, Industrial Exodus (Washington, D. C.: Conference/Alternative State and Local Policies, October 1977), p. 16.

48. Joint Report of Labor Union Study Tour Participants, Economic Dislocation, p. 31.

49. "The easier way out," Economist 272 (August 18, 1979).

50. "Europe: A frantic rush to prop up employment," Business Week, no. 2574 (February 26, 1979): p. 58.

51. Ibid.

52. "Multinational companies," in Kelly and Webb, Plant Closings, pp. 51-52.

53. "Bankruptcy Protection for Employees," World Business Weekly 2 (May 28, 1979): p. 55.

54. C&R Associates, Legislation in Western Europe, p. 66.

55. Canada, Minister of Labor, Redundancies and Lay-Offs, pp. 212-13.

56. S. George Walters and Morris L. Sweet. "Can Private Enterprise Fund and Manage Economic and Social Programs?," paper presented at the October 1978 New England Business and Economic Association Conference; Sweet and Walters, Mandatory Housing Finance Programs; and "Steel," European Communities Commission Background Report, ISEC/B27/79 (London: June 29, 1979).

57. "The easier way out," Economist 272 (August 18, 1979).

58. "Moderating between U. K. labor and management," World Business Weekly 2 (October 8, 1979): p. 64.

59. Don Stillman, "The Devastating Impact of Plant Relocations" in Kelly and Webb, Plant Closings, pp. 41-42.

60. "American jobs: Why so many more?," Economist 271 (April 14, 1979): p. 80.

61. Geoffrey Owen, "European chemical industry's national crutches," World Business Weekly 2 (May 28, 1979): p. 63.

62. Richard B. McKenzie, Restrictions on Business Mobility: A Study in Political Rhetoric and Economic Reality (Washington, D. C.: American Enterprise Institute for Public Policy Research, 1979), p. 60.

63. "The international dimensions of the problems of redundancies and layoffs include the effects of changes in the terms and patterns of international trade and changes in foreign investment." Canada, Minister of Labor, Redundancies and Lay-Offs, p. 20.

PART III

INDUSTRIAL POLICY

9

INDUSTRIAL POLICY AND LOCATION

DEFINING INDUSTRIAL POLICY

A major economic concern of the 1980s in the United States will be the formulation of an overall industrial policy or its counterpart, reindustrialization, [1] and its coordination with location policy. Despite the strong and rapidly growing support for a comprehensive national industrial policy, there have been neither unanimity nor firm legislative proposals on the content. The deep-rooted problems that a policy would have to overcome have been in progress for many years; "just finding answers—let alone implementing them—is destined to command the country's attention for a good part of the 1980s."[2] Current decisions will have repercussions on the nation's economy for many years to come.

Before examining the relationship between industrial policy, reindustrialization, and the revitalization to locational controls, the varying interpretations of the term, industrial policy, or its counterparts should be considered. There is no conclusive definition of industrial policy. "Defining, and refining an industrial policy is destined to be a major and controversial preoccupation of government, labor and business during the next few years."[3] Among proponents of formulating an industrial policy, there is no consensus on what constitutes a proper policy. [4] Despite the differing views, industrial policy should not be thought of as a "buzzword" or ephemeral political slogan but should be given the same serious consideration it has received in Western Europe[5] and is receiving as an issue transcending national boundaries. [6]

In a broad sense one approach to industrial policy consists of selecting specific industrial sectors or product lines, either declining or growing, and concentrating on increasing their productivity and competitiveness. Likely successes and failures are either encouraged or discouraged. Another approach would support improvements in productive capacity and efficiency, and strengthen the industrial base by concentrating investment on infrastructure and capital goods in order to adjust to the high price of energy and the intensified international competition. All federal policies, regulations, expenditures, trade, natural resources, antitrust legislation, and industrial promotion would be oriented toward economic growth through assistance for financing, production, and innovation. The government would furnish loans, guarantees, accelerated depreciation, and tax benefits to encourage savings and investment. Social programs would have reduced priority. These objectives are accomplished without excessive planning and government intervention in the economy. [7] The economic successes of Germany and Japan are cited as models.

In this chapter, industrial policy is used in an overall or synthesizing sense which is aimed at rebuilding the economy. From this perspective, the location factor should transcend the different approaches to industrial policy. The analysis of industrial policy in this chapter is concerned primarily with the locational relationship.

The first indications of a forthcoming industrial policy by President Carter did not specify whether the channeling of investment into declining areas would be a social welfare measure, or one concerned with the productivity and efficiency of industry, or would attempt to be both. [8] However, the message that soon followed indicated that this channeling of investment would attempt to accomplish both goals.

Though lacking precision and detail and dealing with diverse issues, the president's economic message of August 28, 1980 represented the beginning of a political debate on devising a policy of national industrial revitalization.[9] A number of proposals were offered under the category of industrial revitalization. One called for formation of an Economic Revitalization Board selected from industry, labor, and the public. The Board would advise the president on a broad range of issues, including recommendations for establishing an industrial development authority and deciding on its activities. The Board would consider how relevant economic development activities currently within various government agencies could be performed by the authority.[10] Key components were to be liberalized depreciation allowances, investment tax credits, and reduced employer payroll taxes. The depreciation and credit benefits would paradoxically encourage capital intensive investment and negate other initiatives designed to reduce unemployment. These would be across the board and not oriented toward particular regions or sectors.

For distressed areas there would be a supplemental targeted investment credit to provide an additional credit of 10 percent for eligible investment projects in areas of high unemployment. Whether this would be sufficient to attract activities was questionable; business was not compelled to invest in these areas; state and local subsidies in nondistressed areas more attractive to management might offer benefits at a level that was high enough to offset some of the gains from the credits.

The emphasis on broad tax cuts as the primary revitalization measure may be misplaced. This kind of approach overlooks the need for first obtaining information on: the extent of physical and product obsolescence; what has to be done for recovery; and what the costs of such actions will be as they pertain to target sectors and regions. After studying these issues, appropriate programs should be devised.[11] There are too many precedents of legislation being enacted without adequate preliminary study and concern for the ultimate costs and results.

There was no explicit priority or mandate that expenditures on economically-related infrastructure, and research and technological development should go to distressed areas and provide the impetus for self-sustained growth. However, this proposal was the earliest of many that are likely to be forthcoming before a consensus emerges on a long-term industrial policy. The focus was largely on government initiatives. But unless there was a reorientation of corporate policies and practices, any industrial policy relying solely on government actions would fail.

As a presidential candidate Mr. Reagan did not directly address the matter of industrial policy. Major features of his economic policy were tax cuts including accelerated depreciation, budget reductions, and provisions for enterprise zones. Accelerated depreciation presents the greatest potential for reindustrialization or revitalization but it would also offer a stimulus for the construction of facilities in new areas rather than expansion in existing locations. A key omission in the economic policy is a recognition of the need for public investment to rebuild the national and regional deteriorated infrastructure and to complement any proposed increases in private investment. Another omission is the source of capital investment to rebuild the infrastructure of enterprise zones.

The role of public investment as a takeoff point for private investment is illustrated by the situation in the U. S. coal industry. It is now in a position to become a major supplier of the world's energy. But to gain a major share of the world trade in coal, an enormous public and private capital investment in mining, railroads, shipping, and ports is required. Because the domestic coal industry lacks adequate facilities, no major long term export contract has been signed. Public investment is needed for the expansion of ports and dredging of harbors. Regional benefits would accrue to the lagging economies of the Midwest and East from the exploitation of their large coal reserves. Furthermore, depressed industries such as shipbuilding and railroading would be revived. [12] If the domestic economy is to regain its competitiveness, the Reagan administration must consider providing an adequate level of public investment.

Industrial policy emanating from the public sector should coincide with business policies that also have a long-range perspective. A fundamental tenet in the formulation of industrial policy is a long-range view; a strong and enduring economy cannot be composed quickly. [13] Similarly, the movement of industry to optimum locations for purposes of productivity and regional recovery cannot be accomplished quickly. Government can utilize various policies to revitalize regions: coordination and concentration of government procurement (including defense), foreign investment, and infrastructure. Through these policies, the regions in which these facilities are placed could become self-sustaining over a period of time. Depressed regions could be revived and become increasingly attractive to the private sector with a minimum of compulsion or subsidy.

A SELF-SUSTAINING REGIONAL ECONOMY

If the objective of self-sustaining regional economies is attained, there would be no need for special subsidies from the central government that are not available to other regions. Regional economies would have the adaptability to reflect changes in markets and technology by generating compensating activities. They could compete for mobile industry on the basis of the advantages they can offer to business, e.g. a skilled labor force, a well-maintained infrastructure, and the existence of externalities. [14] When industrial policy provides the climate for growth, there would be an increasing tendency for industry to move voluntarily to depressed regions.

A turnaround in the slow growth of the domestic economy cannot come entirely from government efforts—changes in regulation, taxes, and monetary policy—but requires a parallel shift in corporate planning away from the dominance of short-range considerations. Just as government has failed to take a long-range viewpoint, so has large business in the United States been concerned largely with the immediate and not-too-distant future, e.g. short-term profit gains and cost reductions, to the detriment of the extended development of innovation and technological competitiveness. [15]

> Instead of blaming the government for their difficulties,
> the industries might better look at the way they have
> used their resources—
>
> [. . .]

While the Japanese, the Germans and even the Koreans
are nipping at their heels, many American industries
have shown a pathological inability to look toward their
welfare in the long run. It is for this reason that the
"government interference" argument is far too simple. [16]

CHANGES IN THE PRIVATE SECTOR

Rather than considering shutdowns and relocations to be the
norm, corporate management could facilitate industrial policy by
locational decisions that try to keep companies fixed for extended periods. If the ubiquitous public subsidies designed to attract industry
are excluded, a cost calculus would indicate that it is probably prefer-
able for enterprises to retain and expand facilities in existing areas.
The enormous wastage of private and public resources required for
the movement of operations are often of dubious value and could be
better applied to the rebuilding of the lagging U. S. industrial structure.

SPATIAL COMPONENTS OF INDUSTRIAL POLICY

There are many facets to industrial policy but the focus of this
volume is on the spatial relationship as expressed in regional policy.
Location policy has to be considered either as a partner or as a component of industrial policy. If this coordination or confluence is lacking, the contradictory and negating effects put both industrial and
location policy in disarray.

> . . . it is increasingly difficult to speak any more of "re-
> gional policy" in the traditional sense. Instead, there is
> an important regional aspect, or dimension, to each of
> the sub-macro policies . . . notably industrial, agricul-
> tural and manpower policies. Since these policies are not
> primarily determined by considerations of regional balance
> and development, and since the instruments applied can
> have important unintended regional side effects, there can
> be quite serious conflicts and contradictions, both at the
> level of the objectives and at that of policies. Hence the
> need for proper coordination between policies directed to
> achieving the broad long term objectives of regional and
> location policy, and those directed to specific companies,
> industries or types of labor. [17]

Examples of this relationship are found in countries taking a

moderately activist line in their industrial policies by attempting to
promote or help promising ventures frequently within the framework
of regional policies;[18] "as is often the case national policies toward
industry cannot be separated from steps to foster regional development."[19] Legislation can reflect this tendency for industrial and regional policy to merge; for example, Belgium accomplished this in a
single piece of legislation.

> . . . the distinction between "industrial" and "regional"
> policy is often blurred—as is evident in the dual "gen-
> eral" and "regional" character of the 1970 Belgian Law
> [Economic Expansion Law, Government Bill 354, April
> 1970]. Smart politicians have come to realize that the
> continuing development of a region (district or zone) ne-
> cessitates a corresponding restructuring of its economy
> through new industrial, commercial, financial, and man-
> agerial technologies. This requires helping areas that do
> not qualify as underdeveloped under certain criteria or
> that are declining and could well become so, either ab-
> solutely or relatively, if new industries are not brought
> in and if healthy "champion firms" are not further assisted.
> "Regional" policy thus quickly assumes a sectoral
> dimension. And industrial policy itself soon focuses on
> particular industries and even on individual firms, in-
> stead of stressing the improvement of factor markets for
> labor, capital, technology, and entrepreneurship—the
> more classical approach to remedying structural prob-
> lems in a country.
>
> [. . .]
>
> It is likely that land-use planning regulations will
> be used increasingly to bend industry to government plans
> since the state can readily use that instrument either to
> oppose industrial plans or to trade a building permit for
> some desirable contribution to public goals. [20]

A European practitioner in the field of industrial development
points to the overlap between regional and sectoral industrial policy
and the worldwide implications of regional industrial development policy. "It is rather artificial to look only at the sectoral side and not to
take account of the implications of what is happening in regional industrial development policy worldwide today . . . the explosion in this
whole business of regional industrial policy" has probably been "the
most significant single development in industrial policy" in the past
four or five years. He is particularly concerned about the lack of coordination between sectoral and regional aids. [21]

SUBNATIONAL COMPETITION FOR INDUSTRY

A glaring example of the lack of coordination between sectoral and regional aids is the subnational competition within the United States for industry. State and local governments with their plethora of competing programs of financial assistance can negate efforts to establish a rational national industrial and locational policy. The aids negate or cancel out any central government initiatives to improve impacted areas. An economic development official in a central city finds himself as a practitioner "in the midst of an irrational system" not of his making. But he has to do his best for his city "even under irrational systemic conditions." The official states:

> I think it is perfectly ridiculous at the national level, and this is a job for the Congressmen, to have the amount of time, money, and energy spent on attracting industry as is going on in our separate communities and in our States, simply because there is an irrational approach to economic development at the intraregional level. [22]

DE FACTO LOCATIONAL CONTROLS

The efforts to formulate an industrial policy in the United States point to the likelihood of de facto locational controls. Increasing leverage on the geographical distribution of economic activity will come from public decisions on the financial support for certain industries, and investment in social and physical infrastructure. [23] The question is whether the resulting activity will be directed or guided to impacted areas. Without consciousness of the consequences, the spatial pattern of industry could be fixed for years by virtue of decisions made under the aegis of industrial policy. [24] The arrival of a large enterprise brings along other businesses, or increases the profits of those already there who benefit from the linkages or proximity. The external economies needed to serve the new enterprise give the area an advantage over other areas that may be intrinsically better locations but are less developed.

Progress toward a successful industrial policy can be achieved by reducing excessive costs and removing barriers to productivity that accrue from uneconomic locations whether for existing operations or for the placement of new ones. In this connection questions will arise in the formulation of industrial/locational policy. Can various goals be combined: increased efficiency and productivity, improvements in regional and local economies, or social welfare and equity? [25] Will the government assign a lower priority and cut the resources allocated to the rebuilding of inner cities and declining regions where there is a slower return in terms of industrial policy? Will assistance be directed, regardless of geography, to particular sectors and companies with the techniques and products that have the greatest growth potential?[26] What happens to firms in the impacted regions who perform less competitively?

Conceding that there are problems in finding and utilizing suitable measures of efficiency, the cost of raising productivity in the impacted regions may be excessive and thus harmful to national economic growth. But where productivity in impacted regions is equal or potentially equal to productivity in other regions, locational controls (de facto or de jure) can serve to direct industry to impacted regions. These regions should receive preference for new types of activity; there may be too high a price for the diversion of existing industry from areas conducive to productivity and which contain externalities.

A SOCIAL CONTRACT

The participation of business, government, and labor in the form of a social contract is considered a sine qua non if conflicts are to be reconciled and the goals of industrial policy are to be realized;[27] therefore, contravening actions are to be forestalled. Under the Carter proposal, this cooperation would consist of a high-level national board, representing industry, labor, and the public; the board is not enterprise-oriented nor a form of codetermination. Businesses that are hurt in the struggle for new, expanded, or retained facilities could create opposition, especially when communities and workers are adversely affected. Codetermination could elicit the participation of labor in accepting change and could clear the way for the restructuring of firms or industries with a minimum of conflict.[28]

For declining firms and industries using outmoded technologies, plants and equipment, plant-closing legislation can ease the problems of closings or divestments through an adequate system of benefits.[29] Investment can be shifted to new technology and facilities or to operations in the most economic sites.

Programs that appear to be largely negative in nature, i. e. limit the mobility of industry, can have a positive role in industrial policy by facilitating adaptation and change. These programs exemplify the type of instruments that can serve as a bridge between industrial and locational policy and lead to national and regional economic revitalization and growth.

NOTES

1. Gail Garfield Schwartz and Pat Choate, Revitalizing the US Economy: A Brief for National Sectoral Policies (Washington: Academy for Contemporary Problems, 1980); Amitai Etzioni, "Re-Industrialize, Revitalize—Or What?," National Journal 12 (October 25, 1980): 1818; John Pinder, Takashi Hosomi, and William Diebold, Jr., Industrial Policy and the International Economy (New York: Trilateral Commission, 1979); "The Reindustrialization of America," Business Week, no. 2643 (June 30, 1980): 55; and Subcommittee on Industrial Policy and Productivity, Senator Adlai E. Stevenson, chairman, Report in Senate Democratic Task Force on the Economy, Senator Lloyd Bentsen, chairman, Report, September 1980.

2. Arlene Hershman with Mark Levenson, "The 'Reindustrialization' of America?," Dun's Review 116 (July 1980): p. 43.

3. Ibid., p. 34.

4. Robert J. Samuelson, "More Make-work," National Journal 12 (June 7, 1980): p. 944.

5. Steven J. Warnecke and Ezra N. Suleiman, eds., Industrial Policies in Western Europe (New York: Praeger, 1975).

6. William Biebold, Jr., Industrial Policy as an International Issue (New York: McGraw-Hill, 1980).

7. Amitai Etzioni, "Rebuilding our economic foundations," Business Week, no. 2651 (August 25, 1980): p. 16.

8. U.S., President, Office of the White House Press Secretary, Text of the President's Remarks to National Urban League Annual Conference, New York City, August 5, 1980.

9. U.S., President, Office of the White House Press Secretary, "Economic Growth for the 1980's," August 28, 1980.

10. "As federal policy-makers review . . . proposals to stimulate investment within the United States, the positive consequences of broadbrush changes in the nation's tax code may seem apparent. But the benefits may be accompanied by unintended side-effects, with negative implications for distressed communities and even entire regions of the nation. Approaches that more narrowly direct tax incentives to encourage investment may be an effective and fiscally sound way to address the nationwide problems of inadequate capital formation and lagging growth in productivity." Northeast-Midwest Institute, Tax Cuts for Business: Will They Help Distressed Areas? (Washington, D.C.: September 1980), prepared by Mary Fitzpatrick and Peter Tropper, p. 58.

11. "The actual implementation of policies is further complicated by the inability of government bureaucracies to deal with such linkages as technology, capital funding, transportation, energy, land use, and taxation, which are intrinsic to the solution of policy issues.

Instead, each agency deals largely from its perception of need, arising from its community of interest and definition of constituency." Edward Schwartzman, planning consultant, unpublished paper, August 1980.

12. Agis Salpukas, "Hopes for Coal Exports Tied to Investment," New York Times, November 19, 1980, p. 1.

13. ". . . industrial 'regeneration' requires at least a decade if not a generation of forward planning in the sense of requiring a consistent basic strategy." Glyn Davies, "Wales: Japan jumps in while Whitehall hesitates," Business Location File 4 (July 1980): p. 59.

14. N. S. Segal, "The Limits and Means of 'Self-Reliant' Regional Economic Growth," in Duncan Maclennan and John B. Parr, eds., Regional Policy: Past Experience and New Directions (Oxford: Martin Robertson, 1979), p. 212.

15. Robert H. Hayes and William J. Abernathy, "Managing our way to economic decline," Harvard Business Review 58 (July/August 1980): p. 67.

16. James Fallows, "American Industry: What Ails It, How to Save It," Atlantic Monthly 246 (September 1980): pp. 42, 43.

17. Organization for Economic Cooperation and Development, The Case for Positive Adjustment Policies: A Compendium of OECD Documents 1978/79 (Paris: June 1979), p. 115.

18. Ibid., p. 107.

19. Steven J. Warnecke, "Introduction," in Warnecke and Suleiman, eds., Industrial Policies, p. 10.

20. J. J. Boddewyn, "The Belgian Economic Expansion Law of 1970," in Warnecke and Suleiman, eds., Industrial Policies, p. 43.

21. Pinder, Hosomi, and Diebold, Industrial Policy, p. 79.

22. Kenneth E. Fry in U. S., Congress, House of Representatives, Committee on Banking and Currency, Ad Hoc Subcommittee on Urban Growth, Industrial Location Policy: Hearings, 91st Cong., 2d sess., 1970, p. 138.

23. "Today almost all physical infrastructure—the roads, airports, harbors, the gas and electricity installations, the water and drainage systems—is publicly provided. This simple fact makes a mockery of the statement that public planning cannot control market trends." Peter Self, "Whatever happened to regional planning?," Town and Country Planning 49 (July/August 1980): p. 209.

24. "In many respects regional policy per se can only be 'tinkering.' Certainly in terms of the resources involved, regional policy pales into insignificance alongside those national policies which are operated with no explicit spatial component. Unless there is a stronger development of a consciousness of the spatial consequences of national policy, and an attempt to give these policies a spatial orientation, then there can be little doubt that any speedy solution to the regional problem will not be possible. In many countries this point is not recognized,

and indeed there is often not even information available about the spatial distribution of expenditure on 'national' policies." Kevin Allen, Chris Hull, and Douglas Yuill, More Options in Regional Incentive Policy (Berlin: International Institute of Management, March 1979) IIM/79-3, p. 27.

25. Daniel Todd, "Welfare or Efficiency: Can the Growth Center Offer a Compromise?," Growth and Change 11 (July 1980): p. 39.

26. Jan Tinbergen, "What Sectors Should be Stimulated by a Recovery Policy?," Lloyds Bank Review, no. 137 (July 1980): p. 30.

27. Business Week, "Reindustrialization," pp. 86-101.

28. A model for tripartite cooperation of business, labor, and government that has been proposed for the housing industry could serve as a component of industrial policy. Sweet and Walters, Mandatory Housing Finance Programs, pp. 222-23.

29. The Subcommittee on Industrial Policy and Productivity favored increasing the effectiveness of Federal adjustment assistance programs for workers and communities that would facilitate structural change. Subcommittee on Industrial Policy and Productivity, Senator Adlai E. Stevenson, chairman, Report in Senate Democratic Task Force on the Economy, Senator Lloyd Bentsen, chairman, September, 1980, p. 5.

BIBLIOGRAPHY

Advisory Commission on Intergovernmental Relations. Regional
   Growth: Historic Perspective. A-74. Washington, D. C. : Government Printing Office, June 1980.

Agnelli, Giovanni. "Industrial Policy in the European Parliament:
   Problems and Prospects." Europe Brussels no. 986 (February
   9, 1978).

Alexander, Milton. "Gathering Information on Regional Differences
   in Buying." Journal of Commerce. n. d. In Sales Management:
   Theory and Practice. Edited by Milton Alexander and Edward
   M. Mazze. New York: Pitman, 1965, p. 405.

Allen, Kevin, ed. Balanced National Growth. Lexington, Mass. :
   Lexington Books, 1979.

"American Survey: A leaf out of Europe's industrial book." Economist
   276 (August 9, 1980): p. 21.

Alperovitz, Gar, and Faux, Jeff. "Conservative Chic: Reindustrialization." Social Policy 11 (November/December 1980): p. 6.

Anderson, Rob, and Morton, Rosemary. "Place and Chips." Planner
   Britain 65 (1979): p. 98.

Baratta, Paolo. "Public Intervention and Development Policies for
   Southern Italy." Paper presented to Regional Studies Associa-
   tion Conference on Financing of Regional Development in the
   European Economic Community. Dublin, June 1979.

Berentsen, William H. "Regional Policy and Industrial Overspeciali-
   zation in Lagging Regions." Growth and Change 9 (July 1978):
   p. 9.

Berry, A. P. , ed. Worker Participation—The European Experience.
   Coventry, England: Coventry and District Engineering Employers Association, 1974.

Beynon, N. John, and Whysall, Paul T. Planning Issues in the Netherlands: Selected Field Study Notes. Trent Papers in Planning No. 78/4. Nottingham, England: Trent Polytechnic, May 1978.

Boddewyn, J. J. International Divestment: A Survey of Corporate Experience. New York: Business International, 1976.

Boersma, Lotty. Regional Problems and Policies in Europe: A Dutch Bibliography IIM/78-12. Berlin: International Institute of Management, July 1978.

Bowers, J. K. , and Gunawardena, A. "Industrial Development Certificates and Regional Policy. " Bulletin of Economic Research Departments of Economics, Universities of Hull, Leeds, Sheffield, York, and Bradford 29 (November 1977): p. 112; and 30 (May 1978): p. 3.

Brittan, Samuel. "Property rights in jobs. " Financial Times, April 2, 1980, p. 44.

Brown, A. J. , and Burrows, E. M. Regional Economic Problems: Comparative experiences of some market economies. London: George Allen and Unwin, 1977.

Burrell, O. K. "Industrial Adaptation. " Business Topics 7 (Spring 1959). In Readings in Marketing. Edited by S. George Walters, Max D. Snider, and Morris L. Sweet. Cincinnati: South Western, 1962, p. 220.

C&R Associates. Community Costs of Plant Closings: Bibliography and Survey of the Literature. Prepared for the Federal Trade Commission, Contract L0362, July 1978.

____. Measuring the Community Costs of Plant Closings: Overview of Methods and Data Sources. Prepared for Federal Trade Commission, Contract L0458, 1978.

Cameron, Gordon C. "The National Industrial Strategy and Regional Policy. " In Regional Policy: Past Experiences and New Directions. Edited by Duncan MacLennan and John B. Parr. Oxford: Martin Robertson, 1979, p. 297.

Cannon, James B. "Government Impact on Industrial Locations. " In Locational Dynamics of Manufacturing Activity. Edited by Lyndhurst Collins and David F. Walker. London: John Wiley, 1975, p. 109.

Carter, Charles I. "Regional Policy in a Period of Stagnation." Discussion Paper No. 6. London: Regional Studies Association, April 1975.

Chiplin, Brian, and Wright, Mike. "Divestment and Structural Change in UK." National Westminster Bank Quarterly Review (February 1980): p. 42.

Clark, Thomas A. "Regional Development: Strategy from Theory." In Revitalizing the Northeast. Edited by George Sternlieb and James W. Hughes. New Brunswick, N.J.: Rutgers University Center for Policy Research, 1978, p. 407.

Cornelius, Andrew. "Winning foreign aid for development areas." Financial Weekly, July 27, 1979, p. 8.

Cox, Kevin R. A Political Geography of the Contemporary World. Chicago: Maaroufa Press, 1979.

Crowe, Kenneth C. America for Sale. Garden City, N.Y.: Doubleday, 1978.

Diebold, William, Jr. Industrial Policy as an International Issue. New York: McGraw-Hill, 1980.

Drucker, Peter F. "Planning for 'Redundant' Workers." Wall Street Journal, September 25, 1979, p. 28.

Drudy, P.J., ed. Regional and Rural Development: Essays in Theory and Practice. Chalfont St. Giles, England: Alpha Academic, 1976.

Eizenstadt, Stuart E. "A Non-Economist's Look at Economic Policy for the 1980's." Lecture presented to the Alumni Forum, University of North Carolina, Chapel Hill, N.C., May 10, 1980.

Estall, R.C., and Buchanan, R.O. Industrial Activity and Economic Geography. 3rd ed. London: Hutchinson University Library, 1973.

European Communities. Commission. "The Community's Industrial Policy." European File no. 3/79.

European Communities. Economic and Social Committee. How regional development helps to solve unemployment and inflation:

Opinion of the Economic and Social Committee. No. Ex-22-77-435-EN-C, 1977.

European Communities. "Protection of Employees in the Event of the Insolvency of Their Employer." European Communities trade union information no. 5/1979, p. 4.

Franko, Lawrence G. "Industrial Policies in Western Europe—Solution or Problem." World Economy 2 (January 1979): p. 31.

Fry, Earl H. Financial Invasion of the U. S. A. : A Threat to American Society? New York: McGraw-Hill, 1980.

Goddard, J. B. "Technology Forecasting in a Spatial Context." Futures 12 (April 1980): p. 90.

Gordon, Harvey, ed. Economic Conditions Quarterly New York City Department of City Planning 1979-80, passim.

Grady, Susan, and Schneeweis, Thomas. "Legal Environment of Foreign Direct Investment in New England." Paper presented to the New England Business and Economic Conference, Hyannis, Mass. , October 1980.

Great Britain. Department of Industry. The economics of industrial subsidies. Edited by Alan Whiting. London: Her Majesty's Stationery Office, 1976.

Griffiths, Michael. "The Inner City Debate: An Overview." Reading Geographer no. 6 (May 1978): p. 73.

Hansen, Niles M. , ed. Public Policy and Regional Economic Development. Cambridge, Mass. : Ballinger, 1974.

Haskins, Gage B. A. with Miles, Simon R. A Comparative Analysis of the National Urban Growth Policy Experiences of Eight Selected Countries. Prepared for U. S. Dept. of Housing and Urban Development Req. 1920-77. Washington: Fry Consultants, December 1, 1977.

Heathfield, David F. The Economics of Codetermination. London: MacMillan Press, 1977.

Hekman, John S. , and Strong, John S. "Is There a Case for Plant Closing Laws?" New England Economic Review (July/August 1980): p. 34.

Holland, Stuart. The Regional Problem. London: MacMillan Press, 1976.

Hull, Chris. Regional Problems and Policies in Europe: A French Bibliography IIM/78-11. Berlin: International Institute of Management, July 1978.

"Industrial Policy and the International Economy." Trialogue no. 20 (Summer 1979): p. 8.

"Industrial Policy: Mrs. Thatcher's awkward inheritance." Economist 271 (May 5, 1979): p. 120.

Jaeggin, Albert H. "Old Threat to Free Enterprise Back in Congress with New Number." Area Development 12 (March 1977): p. 4.

____. "Your Company's Life Is at Stake." Area Development 14 (November 1979): p. 4.

Japan, Ministry of Finance, International Finance Bureau; and Bank of Japan, Foreign Department, Manual of Foreign Investment in Japan. Tokyo, March 1976.

"Japanese Shopping List for Choosing US Sites Contains Unique Criteria." Business International 27 (June 27, 1980): p. 202.

Jewkes, John. The Control of the Location of Industry in Great Britain. National Economic Problems Series No. 466. New York: American Enterprise Association, 1952.

Johnson, Chalmers. "MITI and Japanese International Economic Policy." In The Foreign Policy of Modern Japan. Edited by Robert A. Scalapino. Berkeley: University of California Press, 1977, p. 227.

Kavanagh, John C. "How Passage of HR-5040 and S-1608 Might Affect You." Area Development 14 (November 1979): p. 6.

Keeble, David. "Industrial Decline in the Inner City and Conurbation." Transactions Institute of British Geographers 3, no. 1 (1978): p. 110.

Knightley, Phillip. "How Datsun built no-permit offices." Sunday Times London, August 29, 1976, p. 2.

Levine, Ted M. "Prenotification—An insidious idea to be stamped out." Area Development 14 (September 1979): p. 94.

Lindley, Jonathan. "The Economic Environment and Urban Development." Lecture presented to the 8th Annual Conference for Economic Projections of the National Planning Association, April 28, 1967, U.S. Department of Commerce, Washington, D.C. In Marketing Management Viewpoints: Commentary and Readings. Edited by S. George Walters, Morris L. Sweet, and Max D. Snider. Cincinnati: South Western, 1970, p. 94.

"Locational Controls on Industry: Development Tool for Impacted Regions in Europe and Japan." Urban Innovation Abroad 2 (March 1978): p. 2.

MacKay, Ross. "The Limits to Regional Policy." Town and Country Planning 45 (October 1977): p. 426.

MacLennan, Duncan, and Parr, John B., eds. Regional Policy: Past Experience and New Directions. Oxford: Martin Robertson, 1979.

Maunder, Peter, ed. Government Intervention in the Developed Economy. London: Croom Helm, 1979.

McCrone, Gavin. Regional Policy in Britain. London: George Allen and Unwin, 1969.

McLoughlin, Peter. "Regional Policy for the Inner City." Reading Geographer Issue no. 6 (May 1978): p. 51.

_____. Regional Policy and the Inner Areas: A Study of Planners' Attitudes Geographical Papers No. 64. Department of Geography, University of Reading, June 1978.

Nicol, William R. "Relaxation and Reorientation: Parallel Trends in Regional Disincentive Policies." Urban Studies 16 (October 1979): p. 333.

Organization for Economic Cooperation and Development. Issues of Regional Policies. Prepared by A. Emanuel. Paris: 1973.

_____. Salient features of regional development policy in Japan. Paris: October 1971.

_____. Restrictive Regional Policy Measures. Prepared by A. Bergan. Paris: 1977.

Paul, Bill. "Director Conflicts Germany's Requiring of Workers on Boards Causes Many Problems." Wall Street Journal, December 10, 1979, p. 1.

Peirce, Neal R., and Steinbach, Carol. "Reindustrialization—A Foreign Word to Hard-Pressed American Workers." National Journal 12 (October 25, 1980): p. 1784.

Pignatelli, Andrea Cendali, and Ronzani, Silvio. Regional Problems and Policies in Europe: An Italian Bibliography IIM/77-3. Berlin: International Institute of Management, May 1977.

Preston, Richard. "Support of HR-76 Suggests Possibility of Cancer." Area Development 13 (November 1978): p. 44.

Radisch, Rhoda. Profile of New York City's Municipal Loan Program. New York City Housing and Development Administration, Office of Programs and Policy Report no. 15, December 1967.

Redburn, F. Stevens, and Buss, Terry F. "Public Policies for Communities in Economic Crisis: An Overview of the Issues." Policy Studies Journal 8 (Autumn 1979): p. 149.

Reuss, Henry S. "A Department of Industry and Trade to Improve Our Economic Structure." In U. S. , Congress. Congressional Record, 96th Cong. , 2d sess. 126 (March 10, 1980): H1687.

Roberts, Benjamin C. , ed. Towards Industrial Democracy. London: Croom Helm, 1979.

Ronzani, Silvio. Background Notes to Regional Incentives in Italy. IIM/78-5d. Berlin: International Institute for Management, March 1978.

Rubenstein, James M. The French New Towns. Baltimore: Johns Hopkins University Press, 1978.

Sacks, Seymour; Hellmuth, Jr. , William F. ; with Egand, Leo. Financing government in a metropolitan area: The Cleveland experience. Glencoe, IL.: Free Press, 1961.

Saxonhouse, Gary R. "The World Economy and Japanese Foreign Economic Policy." In The Foreign Policy of Modern Japan. Edited by Robert A. Scalapino. Berkeley: University of California Press, 1977, p. 281.

Schwartz, Gail Garfield. Urban Economic Development in Great Britain and West Germany: Lessons for the United States. Columbus, Ohio: Academy for Contemporary Problems, 1980.

Shankland, Graeme. "The Next Ten Years." Town Planning Review 48 (July 1977): p. 169.

Sheriff, Tom. A Deindustrialized Britain? Fabian research series 341. London: Fabian Society, March 1979.

Shoup, Carl S. "Taxation in France." National Tax Journal 8 (December 1955): p. 328.

Singh, Inderjit. "New Job Programs to Aid Business." In Economic Conditions Quarterly. New York City Department of City Planning. 2d quarter 1979, p. 1.

Spreiregen, Maurice L. "The Bureau of Planning and Program Research: Functions of a Research Bureau in a Redevelopment Agency." Master's thesis, New York University, 1966.

Summers, Clyde. "American and European Labor Law: The Use and Usefulness of Foreign Experience." Buffalo Law Review 16 (February 1966): p. 221.

Sweet, Morris L. "Codetermination and the Location of Industry in Impacted Regions." Paper presented to the New England Business and Economic Association Conference, Newport, R.I., October 1978.

_____. "Decision Making and French Planning." Business and Government Review 8 (January/February 1967). In Comparative Economic Systems. Edited by Jan Sprybla. New York: Appleton-Century-Crofts, 1969, p. 200.

_____. "How Corporations View British Facility Controls." Area Development 12 (April 1977): p. 16.

_____. Industrial Development in New York City. New York City Housing and Redevelopment Board, Bureau of Planning and Program Research Report No. 10, May 1964.

____. "Industrial Location Policy: Western European Precedents for Aiding U. S. Impacted Regions." Urbanism Past and Present no. 7 (Winter 1978-79): p. 1.

____. "Mandating Industry to Locate in the Northeast." Paper presented to the New England Business and Development Conference, Wakefield, Mass., November 1977.

____. "The Role of Tax Exemption in Industrial Development." Area Development 14 (February 1967): p. 36.

____. "State Plant Closing Legislation." Paper presented to New England Business and Economic Conference, Boston, October 1979.

____. "State and Local Government Loans for Industrial Development." Journal of Business Seton Hall University 6 (December 1967): p. 13.

Sweet, Morris L., and Walters, S. George. Mandatory Housing Finance Programs: A Comparative International Analysis. New York: Praeger, 1976.

____. "Global companies take big steps: Establishing an overseas base." Printer's Ink 287 (May 29, 1964): p. 259.

Sweet, Morris L., and Jensen, Finn B. "The Planned Community." National Civic Review 51 (May 1962). In Marketing Management Viewpoints: Commentary and Readings. Edited by S. George Walters, Morris L. Sweet, and Max D. Snider. 2d ed. Cincinnati: South Western, 1970, p. 71.

Tabb, William K. "Government Incentives to Private Industry to Locate in Urban Poverty Areas." Land Economics 45 (November 1969): p. 392.

Therkildsen, Ole. "Regional Development in Western Europe: A Study of the Locational Behavior of Large Industrial Enterprises." Master's thesis. Cornell University, January 1977.

Torem, Charles, and Craig, William Laurence. "Control of Foreign Investment in France." Michigan Law Review 66 (February 1968): p. 669.

Travis, Paul A., and Schoeps, Dan. "The Impact of Military Spending." CONEG Northeast Report 1 (August 27, 1978): p. 4.

Turner, D. Michael. "Location Decisions of IDC Policy in the United Kingdom." In Spatial Perspectives on Industrial Organization and Decision Making. Edited by F. E. Ian Hamilton. London: John Wiley, 1974.

Umrath, Heinz. European Labor Movements and Housing. Brussels: European Regional Organization of the International Confederation of Free Trade Unions, 1963.

U. S. , Congress, Congressional Budget Office. Economic Conversion: What Should Be The Government's Role? January 1980.

U. S. , Congress, Joint Economic Committee. Environmental and Health/Safety Regulations, Productivity Growth, and Economic Performance: An Assessment, 96th Cong. , 2d sess. , August 1980.

United Nations Development Programme. The Need for Industrial Restructuring by Industrialized Countries. Prepared by Jan van Ettinger. Development Issue Paper for the 1980s. no. 6, 1980.

"US Industrial Policy Is Fraught With Difficulty And a Long Way Off." Business International 27 (August 8, 1980): p. 249.

Wallace Andrew M. "Toward Economic Revitalization: Conversions Restore Old Plants, Create Jobs with U. S. , State Aid." World of Work Report 5 (October 1980): p. 1.

Walters, S. George, and Sweet, Morris L. "Lessons from France in Housing Finance." Urban Innovation Abroad 2 (May 1978): p. 2.

____. "Can Private Enterprise Manage Economic and Social Programs?" Paper presented to New England Business and Economic Association Conference, Newport, R. I. , October 1978.

Walters, S. George, Sweet, Morris L. , and Snider, Max D. "When Industry Moves to Interurbia." Sales Management 82 (February 20, 1959). In Marketing Management Viewpoints: Commentary and Readings. Edited by S. George Walters, Morris L. Sweet, and Max D. Snider. Cincinnati: South Western, 1970, p. 89.

Warnecke, Steven J. , and Suleiman, Ezra, eds. Industrial Policies in Western Europe. New York: Praeger, 1975.

Whysall, Paul T. "Regional Economic Planning in the Netherlands."
Town and Country Planning 48 (November 1979): p. 263.

Wynne, George G. , ed. Survival Strategies: Paris and New York.
New Brunswick, N. J. : Transaction Books, 1979.

Zysman, John. Political Strategies for Industrial Order, State, Market, and Industry in France. Berkeley: University of California
Press, 1977.

INDEX

AFL-CIO (American Federation of Labor and Congress of Industrial Organizations), 106 (see also unions)

Agrément, 53–57 (see also France)

agriculture, 61, 63, 85, 128–29

Airline Pilots Association, 107

Akso, 141

Alcoa, 75

Alpha Carbide, 127

American Motors Corporation (AMC), 108, 119

Anheuser Busch, 107

Ashcroft, Brian, 43

assisted areas, 89, 98; in France, 55–57; in Great Britain, 20–51 [development, 20, 28, 30, 31, 33–37; intermediate, 20; special development, 20–21, 28, 44–45, 47]; in the United States, 27 (see also declining areas; depressed areas; distressed areas; impacted areas)

Association of Metropolitan Authorities, 97

Australia, foreign investment in, 79–82

Authorization, 57–61 (see also Italy)

automobile industry, 60–61 (see also individual manufacturers)

bankruptcy, 128, 130, 136, 139, 142

BAT Industries, 137–38

Belfast, 65

Belgium, 142, 158

Bergsten, C. Fred, 90

Biedenkopf, Kurt, 114

Biedenkopf Commission, 114–15, 120–21 (see also codetermination; unions; West Germany)

Birmingham, 28, 35, 46–48

Bristol, 33–37, 38–39

British Redundancy Payments Act of 1965, 135–36 (see also redundancy pay; unemployment, pay for)

Brown, A. J., 42–43

Burroughs, 30

Canada, 74, 90, 133–34, 143; foreign investments in, 76–79

Canada Manpower Consultative Service, 143

Carter, Jimmy, 154, 160

cash trade adjustment allowance, 131 (see also unemployment, pay for)

Chrysler, 107–8, 108–9, 140

cities, 9, 27, 52–57, 63–64, 97–98; in Great Britain, 20, 33, 46–47; in the United States, 9, 11, 159, 160 (see also individual cities)

ABOUT THE AUTHOR

MORRIS L. SWEET has been affiliated since 1975 with the New York City Department of City Planning as a principal planner in the Division of Economic Planning and Development. He was previously a senior staff member of the New York City Housing and Development Administration in a research and analysis capacity. Prior to joining the New York City government, he was connected with Lehigh University as a research assistant professor of business. He has served as a consultant to public and private organizations, conducting studies on industrial, commercial, and residential development. His primary interests are in policies and programs related to economic and industrial development.

His published work has appeared in books, papers, monographs, and articles in professional and technical journals. He is the coauthor and coeditor of Marketing Management Viewpoints: Commentary and Readings, South Western, 1970 and coauthor of Mandatory Housing Finance Programs: A Comparative International Analysis, Praeger, 1976. His undergraduate work in economics was done at Rutgers University and he received an M. B. A. from the New York University Graduate School of Business Administration. He is a member of United States and foreign professional societies in the fields of economics, public administration, and regional and urban planning.